CONNECTICUT
BOOTLEGGER QUEEN
NELLIE GREEN

CONNECTICUT
BOOTLEGGER QUEEN
NELLIE GREEN

TONY RENZONI

Foreword by Charlene Green Massey

THE
History
PRESS

Published by The History Press
Charleston, SC
www.historypress.com

Copyright © 2021 by Anthony Renzoni
All rights reserved

Unless otherwise noted, all images are from the collection of Charlene Green Massey, the great-granddaughter of Nellie Green.

First published 2021

Manufactured in the United States

ISBN 9781467147934

Library of Congress Control Number: 2020951988

This book is lovingly dedicated to the family of Nellie Green Talmadge.

CONTENTS

FOREWORD

As the great-granddaughter of Nellie Green, it is a privilege and honor for me to write the foreword for Tony Renzoni's wonderful book on Nellie titled *Connecticut Bootlegger Queen Nellie Green*.

I am proud of the legacy she has left us—a legacy of kindness, generosity, humanity, courage, honesty and integrity. And yes, Nellie has passed down to her family, including me, her lifelong principles of hard work and fearlessness.

A devoted daughter, wife, and grandmother, Nellie made it known to all that, in her mind, family always came first. Her unconditional love for her family was never so evident than in the steadfast love and devotion shown to her polio-stricken son Charlie. His illness and death had a profound effect on Nellie. She invested a great deal of time and depleted her hard-earned money to care for her son. And yet she would have it no other way. This was a life lesson for our entire family.

Early on, Nellie became a living legend in Connecticut. Her courageous acts touched the lives of so many people in the Connecticut area. People from East Haven and Branford never forgot her selfless acts of courage in saving so many people from drowning in the Farm River.

Once Prohibition took place, Nellie conducted her bootlegging operation in an open, forthright and honest manner. There was mutual love between Nellie and the people of East Haven. She earned their respect and cooperation as the proprietor of the Hotel Talmadge. In fact, many of her neighbors were her most frequent customers at the hotel.

Nellie was a very independent woman who possessed an astute business sense. She had a perceptive instinct about people and was tough toward individuals who did not have her best interest at heart. Her toughness helped her to hold her own in the male-dominated world that existed at that time.

I am very proud of my great-grandmother's accomplishments and the sense of love and devotion she has passed down to my entire family.

I wish to thank Tony Renzoni for his thorough research. I highly recommend this book and his tribute to a remarkable person—my great-grandmother Nellie Green.

—Charlene Green Massey,
great-granddaughter of Nellie Green

ACKNOWLEDGEMENTS

I am very appreciative to all the people who have shared their knowledge, provided valuable insight and, above all, offered great support to me and this endeavor. Grateful acknowledgements to Charles W.G. Talmadge III, Colleen Renzoni, Dr. Kerry Renzoni, Dan Mancinone, Karen Mancinone, Mary Blacker, Bruce Loman, Alice and Don Schwartz, Anne Killheffer, Bob Cullum, Elizabeth Clemens, Jane Bouley, Jenna Anthony, Mary Winter, Maryalice Hoogland, Molly Banes, Pam Graham Dolin, Peter Cameron, Rhoda Winik and the U.S. Coast Guard. A special thank-you to Charlene Green Massey for providing many of the photos in this book. And a big thank-you to Karen Mancinone for her assistance with some of the photos. Finally, I wish to thank my book publisher (Arcadia Publishing/The History Press) and, of course, editors Abigail Fleming and Mike Kinsella for all their wonderful guidance and support during this entire book process.

INTRODUCTION

Before I knew it, I was makin' more money than I knew what to do with. It was then I realized that good ole Honorable Andrew J. Volstead was the goose that was laying the golden eggs, and I had no intention of interfurin' with that!
—Nellie Green, legendary Connecticut bootlegger

At a very early age, Nellie Green was very much influenced by her father's words that morality cannot be legislated. This applied to gambling on roosters, prizefights and horses. And when she was forty-seven years old, it applied to bootlegging liquor.

Nellie was a prominent and successful bootlegger who received a great deal of cooperation and support from many people throughout the Connecticut area. These are people who witnessed firsthand Nellie's kindness, generosity and courage. They were also very much aware of the fact that Nellie had risked her own life in saving over twenty people who faced certain death from drowning in the frequently violent Farm River where Nellie's hotel was located.

In an age when women were often marginalized, Nellie fearlessly stood up to all those who tried to stand in her way. Like other noted female bootleggers such as Cleo Lythgoe and Willie Carter Sharpe, Nellie was an independent woman who conducted her activities in a fearless, no-nonsense manner and with a keen business sense.

Financial backing for her bootlegging operation came from bankers, merchants, politicians and even prominent members of local and state law enforcement. Together with the unwavering and resolute support from her many loyal customers, Nellie built a lucrative bootlegging empire.

Nellie Green was very much aware that her bootlegging activities were in opposition to the national Prohibition Act. But, much like the famed rumrunner Bill McCoy, Nellie conducted herself, and her business, in an honorable and decent manner.

Nellie's main bootlegging establishment was the Hotel Talmadge. However, she also operated the Dyke House Inn, the Driftwood and the Number 1 House. These establishments were all located on her vast premises in East Haven, Connecticut. And all four places were used at one time or another to serve the growing demand for alcoholic beverages during the Prohibition era.

Nellie's rumrunners were fearless, mysterious men who assumed aliases such as "Blackie," "Wing" and "King Tut." They were men of intrigue, and their compelling exploits are also detailed in this book. Her nine rumrunner boats were so fast that they easily outran the best Coast Guard cutters that were available at the time. All of this earned Nellie Green the title of the "Queen of the Fastest Rumrunners on the East Coast."

One of the greatest research gifts that an author can receive, especially when the book's central figure passed away long before the book is written, is to have access to material written in the central figure's own words. For me, this gift comes in the form of Nellie Green's personal written accounts. I was very fortunate to receive permission from Nellie Green's great-granddaughter Charlene Massey and her family to include in this book as many excerpts from Nellie's written accounts as I felt were needed. For this I am very grateful.

In this book you will read Nellie's personal, detailed account of her life from ten years old up until shortly before her death in 1951. Nellie speaks openly and honestly of her amazing and tumultuous life—before, during and after her bootlegging career. Readers will gain valuable insight into the mindset of this renowned bootlegger as well as her contemporary bootleggers and rumrunners. This is a story of heroism, adventure, humor, excitement and tragedy.

Join me in a journey of the captivating life and times of this legendary figure—set against the historical backdrop of the turbulent Prohibition era, the women's movement and the Roaring Twenties. Nellie Green was, indeed, a living legend.

1

THE EARLY YEARS

I shall call her "Sugar"
—Charles Green

It was 2:00 a.m., and "Wing" St. Clair and his crew were preparing to set out from East Haven's Farm River—destination Rum Row. For this mission, Wing chose to ride on one of his boss's favorite boats, the *Eda*.

Anxious to move on, St. Clair yelled out to his crew, "C'mon men, let's get going. We need to load up our boats and be back before the light of day." As they had done on numerous occasions, Wing and his crew would venture out on the open seas to pick up their cargo from a waiting mothership stationed at the edge of international waters. They would then motor their speedy boats back to Farm River and deliver their precious cargo to the bootlegger who employed them. They were expert navigators, and they were fearless. They had to be. The men were rumrunners, and they were dealing with the dangerous transportation of illegal liquor during the historic era known as Prohibition. St. Clair knew it was important to travel in the wee hours of the morning to avoid the suspicious eyes of the U.S. Coast Guard. The crew knew they were able to outrun the best boats that the Coast Guard had to offer (as they had done many times), but why take further chances? Besides, their boss forbade them from carrying weapons during their missions, so setting out in the early morning made sense to them. These rumrunners knew it was a risky business, but to a man, they

Ten-year-old "Sugar" digging for clams near Farm River.

were more than up to the task. Their boss was tough but fair. Each man was treated as family, and they were all paid handsomely for their efforts. They always made an effort to deliver their goods in a safe and timely manner. It was important to them that they pleased their boss—the bootlegger who owned and managed the speakeasy hotel in East Haven. The bootlegger they worked for was a woman by the name of Nellie Green.

Nellie Adeline Green was born in New Haven, Connecticut, on September 30, 1873, the only child of Charles Green and Ellen E. Glass.

Nellie's grandfather John Green was the son of an English sea captain. He owned around 750 acres adjacent to the Farm River in East Haven, Connecticut. Nellie's father, Charles Green, was born in May 1845. Charles and his father, John, enlisted in the Civil War and served in the Sixth Connecticut Regiment. Charles was only fifteen years old when he enlisted. Charles actually tried to enlist twice before but was turned down because of his age. But he was persistent, and on his third attempt, Charles was permitted to enlist along with his father, John. Captain Gerish, who accepted him, said of Charles, "He is so persistent he will make a good soldier, and I think his father and I together ought to be able to help keep him out of trouble." But Charles was a restless and a mischievous boy. His father and commanding officer were not always successful in keeping him out of mischief, but the tricks he would play on others were innocent and harmless.

Charles served as a teenage drummer boy in the Civil War. He was involved in every battle that his regiment engaged in and never refused an assignment. When the bugle sounded for battle, he was always one of the first to take his position in the formation designated by the military officer. According to media reports, Charles was the first soldier from Connecticut to carry a flag of truce to the enemy. Carrying a flag of truce was a dangerous and courageous act. During the Civil War, soldiers would wave a white flag as a signal to the enemy to stop firing while fallen comrades were removed from a battlefield. While both sides agreed to the white flag, there was a great deal of apprehension and uncertainty that some enemy soldiers would not abide by this agreement.

After one heavily fought battle, young Charles went missing for three days and was given up for dead. On the following day, the fifteen-year-old marched into camp with two prisoners of war and received a hero's welcome for his bravery.

During the war, Charles received multiple wounds in his wrist, knee and legs. During one mission, Charles received a wound that would have a lifelong effect. It was during that mission that Charles was struck in the forehead by a ricocheting Minié ball fired by an enemy rifle. The ball left a permanent indentation in his forehead. For this injury, Charles received extensive hospital treatment for three months. According to many people who knew him, the wound left an even deeper internal psychological scar that accounted for his hot temper and sometimes irrational behavior.

Nellie's mother, Ellen Elizabeth Glass, was born in Glasgow, Scotland, in March 1837. She was a well-educated, sophisticated woman and, according to Nellie, "a great reader in general." Charles and Ellen married in 1870. Like her husband, Nellie's mother was not afraid to show her displeasure and anger when it was called for—especially toward men who drank too much and used foul language. This aversion to strong language and drunkenness was passed on to her daughter and caused many altercations between Nellie and intoxicated individuals who Nellie felt could cause her harm.

Nellie's parents, Ellen (Glass) and Charles Green (looking closely at his forehead, you can see the bullet indentation from his Civil War injury).

EAST HAVEN–SHORT BEACH BRIDGE 1880
OVER FARM RIVER 2nd BRIDGE

Original Farm River bridge and Dyke House (in distance), 1880.

Around 1872, John Green built a place at the foot of Snake Hill in East Haven that became known as the Dyke House Inn. The Dyke House sat directly on the water, where the narrow Farm River divides Branford (Connecticut) and East Haven. For a time, Charles, Ellen and Nellie lived at 110 Prospect Road in East Haven when Nellie was eight years old. The family then moved into the Dyke House, where Nellie recalls growing up: "It had an open porch and served as a public place for clam bakes and the likes of that. My father became the owner and manager of the Dyke House Inn, which became lodging for folks travelin' through. My grandfather sold booze at the Dyke House and people drove from New Haven and the Naugatuck Valley to buy the likker there."

In 1874, soon after the Dyke House was constructed, John Green died. When Charles first heard that his wife had given birth to a girl, he walked into the room and showed his displeasure, having wanted a son. But upon seeing the baby, he changed his mind. Taking baby Nellie in his arms for the first time, Charles said, "I shall call her 'Sugar.'" It was a nickname that stuck.

Even though he reluctantly accepted the fact that Nellie was a girl, Charles was determined to bring her up as a tomboy. When Sugar was only ten years old, Charles began giving her daily boxing lessons to be

Get-together at the Dyke House Inn.

able to defend herself, in his words, "against all comers." Nellie's mother vehemently disapproved, but Charles ignored his wife's opposition. Every day before breakfast, for six years, Charles gave her lessons on boxing and self-defense. As Nellie recalled, "He'd give me a whack, good and hard just to get me mad. My mother, who was a good and refined woman, said it was wrong what he was doin', but she couldn't do nawthin' with him once he got goin'. I guess nobody could."

The lessons would last for six years, until Nellie was sixteen years old:

On my sixteenth birthday, my father approaches me with his boxing gloves darin' me to hit him. My mother called out to him to stop it, sayin' "Sugar's a young lady now and you shouldn't carry on like this anymore." But it didn't do no good. He gave me a good whack, and another and another, right and left. Then I got mad—that is what he was after—and I let him have it. It's the God's honest truth. I punched him all over the room until he gave up. We never put the gloves on after that. I guess he was more than satisfied that I could take care of myself because when he put the gloves away—and

I noticed he was a-puffin'—he said, "Now don't ever let me hear nawthin' from nobody about my daughter."

This was the world in which young Nellie Green was brought up—a physical, rough-and-tumble life. Nellie soon became adept at handling herself with her fists. For good or ill, Nellie would put her physical prowess to good use later in life.

Like her father, Nellie would use her fists and strength when she felt they were needed. Nellie recalled an incident when she was only ten years old, between her and a student at the Short Beach public school:

These kids began pushin' me in the school hallway and I pushed 'em back. Then one of the kids throw'd water on me and that was it. I wrench'd the dipper away from the kid who done it and gave him a hard whack over the head with it. The teacher ran out of the classroom and said "What's goin' on here?" But when she seen me, she smiled, turned her head, and went back into the classroom. The teacher always—all the while I was there, till I was sixteen—made me the monitor while she was out. I was always the monitor.

Sugar was also assigned the task of monitoring the popular but illegal rooster prize fights that her father arranged. They were held in a big gray barn next to the Dyke House. Men from New Haven and other towns would show up, pay a small fee to her father and place their bets on these fighting roosters. (Sugar called them "chickens.") These were no small events, as the barn could accommodate up to two hundred men.

They were tough, fightin' chickens, trained and imported from Ireland. All the big shots—lawyers, bankers, businessmen, and the likes would sneak into the barn to gamble. If any ladies showed up, they'd get throw'd into the river. Honest truth. If the police showed up, it was my job to grab all the chickens and take them as far away as possible. In those days, the river came right up to the back of the barn. All I had to do was grab all the chickens, shove off, and row like hell down the river till things quieted down."

At a very early age, Sugar learned to ride and race the horses that her family owned. When she was only ten years old, Sugar was assigned a number of tasks normally reserved for adults. One such task was to run errands to New Haven with the family's horse and wagon.

On extreme left of this photo is the barn where Sugar monitored the illegal rooster fights (view from Branford).

My father instructed me to ride to New Haven for the purchase of jugs or barrels of whiskey and kegs of beer, ten or fifteen cases of stuff. He would give me a list and tell me to hitch up the horse and go get it. And so, I would hitch up our horse Kit to the wagon and off I'd go. Kit was a sorrel mare, a female horse, and how she would race down the road. And I would not let anyone outrun ol' Kit and me. If another horse and wagon came along and got close, I would put Kit into high gear. I used to sit right up there on the seat—there was no dashboard in front—and I'd hold her tight until the other horse came alongside. Then I would tap Kit with my foot and, oh boy how she would charge down the road. She'd make 3 minutes on that cobbled East Haven road, and she would keep it up. Kit would sweat but didn't seem to tire out. I might 'ave killed her but you know how kids are. Because of the races, Papa's beer would get all foamed up. He'd have to ice it to draw it off, and he'd yell the daylights out of me.

At age sixteen, Nellie felt obliged to leave school (when her mother began losing her sight) and lend a hand in the management of Dyke House. Nellie took control of the neglected family household. Through her own self-discipline and strict attention to finances, Nellie converted the Dyke House Inn into a productive enterprise.

As a child, she helped out by tending the nearby drawbridge that crossed the Farm River into Branford and also delivered lunches to the laborers upstream at the Trap Rock Quarry. She also became more active in the finances and management end of the business.

Nellie's mother's attitude toward abusive language and intoxication was deeply ingrained in her daughter's mind. Throughout her teenage years and even later in life, Nellie was involved in *numerous* confrontations involving intoxicated men using abusive language who made unwanted advances. In a July 1892 incident covered by local news, eighteen-year-old Nellie was approached by an intoxicated young man who made advances toward her. The two engaged in a bloody fistfight, and the man pulled out a knife and stabbed Nellie in the stomach. For this incident, the young man was fined and sentenced to two months in jail.

Nellie Green.

Another altercation that was also covered by the printed media, but on a wider scale, occurred in May 1902. After this incident, twenty-eight-year-old Nellie and another individual (a Mr. Brown) accused each other of assault, with the matter ending up in court. Nellie knew this person quite well. When she was ten years old, she witnessed a fight between Brown and her father. During that altercation, Brown stabbed her father with a knife. Afterward, Charles Green was bedridden for three months. Brown did not fare much better—he was beaten to the ground quite severely by Green.

Nellie described her later confrontation with Brown to the jury this way:

> *Mr. Brown came into the Hotel stinkin' drunk and began to use bad language against me. I told him to shut up or I would beat him along. He then went out to the barn and started drinking whiskey again. I followed him to the barn because I didn't want anything stolen. I told Brown to get out and then he reached in his pocket as if to get a knife. I told him he couldn't stab me in the back like he did my father. Then I kicked him up the hill. After he threw a stone at me, I picked up my stick. I hit him with my stick several times, dropped the stick, and began to use my fists on Mr. Brown.*

The "stick" that Nellie referred to was actually a long riding crop (cane) she was known to carry with her at all times as a defensive weapon. After being treated by a physician for multiple wounds, Brown was fined and sentenced to sixty days in jail.

Nellie's quick temper and unwillingness to walk away from a potential confrontation led to other altercations—sometimes avoidable confrontations—as was the case in a 1906 breach of peace arrest that resulted in a twenty-day prison sentence (which was eventually dismissed). Other breach of peace charge allegations were leveled against Nellie, usually with the judge deciding against the individuals making the allegations after witnesses testified that Nellie was justifiably defending herself.

2

NELLIE'S SINGING AND EQUESTRIAN CAREERS

On Sundays, I would sing religious music in church in the morning and then go back to the Dyke House and sell rum in the afternoon. That's how it was.
—Nellie Green

NELLIE'S SINGING CAREER

The men on the banks or the bridge—I wasn't paying no attention to any of 'em—would go to my father and say "My, what a glorious voice Sugar has! You ought to do somethin' about it."

—Nellie Green

One of Nellie's passions was singing. She once had a very promising singing career. But, as you will soon see, there were obstacles in her life that had a profound and negative influence on her career. It was these obstacles that she could not (or would not) be able to overcome.

At the age of fourteen, Sugar, as noted by her neighbors and friends, was a very attractive girl "with hair the color of molasses." One of her favorite things to do (and a way to avoid the chaos that was part of her upbringing back at home) was to find a serene place and sing while looking out to nature that surrounded the Farm River. She would especially savor those special moments when she would take her rowboat out on the river, pull in her oars

Nellie Green (*standing*) during her singing career in Washington, D.C. (Carry Kennedy, seated).

at sunrise or sunset and just sing out loud. "Lead Me Kindly Light" was always one of her favorites. "A beautiful hymn." As Nellie recalled,

> *Driving my wagon with my horse Kit through the woods at moonlight, I would sing "Ave Maria." I never thought nawthin' about it, only I'd open up and sing just because I felt like it. The men on the banks or the bridge or whichever—I wasn't paying no attention to any of 'em—would go to my father and say "My, what a glorious voice Sugar has! You ought to do somethin' about it."*

According to Nellie, her father also had an untrained, extraordinary voice. "My, but it was beautiful! My father had a tenor voice and it was a gift. I guess I inherited his voice." Her father did as the men on the banks suggested—he arranged for Sugar to receive formal voice lessons. Charles arranged for Sugar to have weekly voice lessons from Ella Mae Belden, who was a soloist at New Haven's Saint Paul's Church and had a great deal of concert experience as well. Sugar's first public singing experience was at age sixteen when she performed at New Haven's Loomis Temple of Music. She won first prize in a competition there. Nellie also performed at Yale University's Woolsey Hall (New Haven, Connecticut). Seeing a good deal of potential in her student, Belden sent Nellie to further her studies under Professor Leopold. Nellie remembered, "He had a studio in an insurance building on Chapel Street in New Haven." He also recognized Nellie's singing potential, telling her, "Your voice is a true and superior mezzo soprano."

Nellie's goal was to have a career on the concert stage, singing in front of large audiences. She received encouragement from both her father and her first husband, Charles Hinckley. "Charles told me 'Sugar, you go right along and if you get any job singing you go right along'. He wouldn't ever let me sing for just anybody who came into Dyke House Inn. They always should be somebody important." Knowing that she needed to expand on her public experience before pursuing a major singing career on stage, Sugar performed at many small local events and larger public ceremonies such as the dedication of the Blackstone Memorial Library in Branford in 1896. Her performances were well received with many requests for encores.

After several years studying under vocal teachers in New Haven, Nellie set her sights on New York. One person who encouraged her to go to New York and find a "backer" was Nellie's longtime friend, famous author and poet Ella Wheeler Wilcox. From 1891 until she died in 1919, Ella lived on

Loomis Temple of Music, New Haven, Connecticut. *Photo by Joseph K. Bundy, the J. Paul Getty Museum.*

Branford's Short Beach coast overlooking Granite Bay and was a regular guest at Nellie's East Haven Inn. Ella gained national fame for her works, including the 1883 collection *Poems of Passion and Solitude*, which contains the lines "Laugh, and the world laughs with you; weep, and you weep alone." According to Nellie: "Ella said I should go to New York and stay at the Waldorf Hotel on Fifth Avenue so I can meet some important people and get me a 'backer.' I tole her I didn't need no backer, I'd back myself. I had plenty of money of my own. But she was insistent and so I went to New York carryin' a letter of introduction from Mrs. Wilcox."

Ella Wheeler Wilcox. *Library of Congress*.

Nellie continued,

In New York, I met with theater owner Tony Pastor, who was famous for promotin' the career of the famous actress and singer Lillian Russell. I sang for Mr. Pastor and he liked my voice. But, for some reason, he didn't like my association with Ella Wilcox and tole me he would consider me singin' at his theater if I would keep away from Mrs. Wilcox. What he said about Ella made me real mad and I tole him straight up that I had no use for him. I called him a stinkpot and left to go back to my place on Farm River. But I kept on singin' in New Haven and other parts. On Sundays, I would sing religious music in church in the morning and then go back to the Dyke House Inn and sell rum in the afternoon. That's how it was.

On a number of occasions, Nellie was invited to sing at prestigious events in Washington, D.C. As Nellie tells it: "I was invited to sing at big parties in Washington—they were private—given by big shot senators and congressmen. That's when I heard that my first husband Charles had been in a serious boating accident."

Nellie returned to New York for an audition with the famed Whitney Opera Company, which was touring with the musical *When Johnny Comes Marching Home.*

> *Mr. Whitney himself gave me tryouts between the acts. He liked what he heard, and the audience applauded and gave me a good reception. Based on my performances, Mr. Whitney said he was interested in givin' me a part in the play. But one night after the show, one of the musicians approached me and started gettin' real personal with me, if you know what I mean. When he wouldn't stop his advancements, I pasted him over the head with my umbrella which was short and I broke it off, and then I used the handle and finished him off with my fists.*

Nellie continued:

> *The next day Mr. Whitney said to me "Nellie, as a friend who has your interest at heart, I wonder how far you'll get if you keep at it professionally. You got a glorious voice, it's natural, and you've got the power that goes with it, and with more trainin' and cultivatin', it can be jest what is needed on the concert stage." He was right about that. I could throw it any place in the Hall, no matter how big. But then he said, "But you've jest got to make concessions to get along in New York where the competition is so stiff. You see, my dear, in a big city like New York we jest can't keep all the people in their places. You've got to learn how to get along with people, all kinds— and you got to learn how to handle them." Well, thinking I knew what he meant—nice and kind as he was—I knew I wasn't making no concessions along that line to nobody. And so, I left and went back to East Haven.*

Later on, Nellie had another opportunity to land a role in a major musical. The famed Henry W. Savage Opera Company arrived in New Haven for performances of *The Redfeather* opera at the Hyperion, a two-thousand-seat auditorium. Nellie once again was given the opportunity to perform between acts as a tryout for a role in *The Redfeather*. Nellie's performances in between acts were well received by the audiences. As Nellie remembered,

> *Mr. Savage liked what he heard and offered me a minor role in the play once the company left New Haven and would perform the play in New York. I was ready to accept the part. But it was then that I received word that my mother was really failin' and goin' blind. Knowin' that I was needed back at Farm River, I decided not to take the part and left for East Haven.*

Ellen (Glass) Green) upon losing her sight, forced Nellie to forego her singing career.

And so, Nellie's promising singing career and her goal of performing on a large concert stage came to a sudden end.

There is little doubt that Nellie possessed a fine, natural signing voice. Aside from her devotion to her family, it all seemed to come down to this unfortunate truth: The opportunities of realizing her goal were fatally stymied and overcome by certain shortcomings in her life imposed on Nellie—and sometimes imposed *by* Nellie. These obstacles included her quick temper, belligerence, and her deep distrust in some people's motives.

NELLIE'S EQUESTRIAN LIFE

An expert rider, Nellie Green was considered one of the finest horseback riders in Connecticut.

Nellie's other lifelong passion was her love for horses. For as long as she could remember, horses were part of her life. When she was only ten years old, Sugar would ride her horse Kit (a reddish-brown female horse) throughout the premises. As previously mentioned, Sugar would hitch Kit up to her wagon numerous times and ride to New Haven to pick up cases of whiskey and beer for her father. Another favorite was her horse Tom.

> *I had a very fine sulky* [horse cart]—*my, but it was a beauty!—and a horse, Tom, which was quite a stepper, I'll say! The people in the towns I drove in used to call me "The lady with the fine sulky." Many times I*

Royal Flush with William Talmadge II aboard.

Sugar's horse Kit (a bit older).

Sugar's horse Tom.

would ride my beautiful sulky and ol' Tom down to Branford and places like that to drum up business for the Dyke House Inn. And business at the Dyke House bar would pick up again.

Bedecked in her trademark long riding coat and derby hat and carrying a riding crop, Nellie was a frequent visitor of nearby towns such as Branford (which bordered East Haven), where she would ride around town in her fancy buggy for business or pleasure. Nellie was quite an attraction for Branford residents as she rode her fabled horse cart on thoroughfares such as Montowese Street, Pine Orchard Road and Main Street.

She eventually assembled a stable of Thoroughbred show horses on a Branford farm she bought. Nellie's prize mount was Royal, Flush "a refined and elegant Saddlebred." The Saddlebred has been called the "world's most beautiful horse" by many horse experts. Royal Flush was featured in the nationally recognized *Riders and Drivers* magazine, which noted: "The three-gaited horse is the epitome of beauty, grace and elegance. A horse in this class does not have to perform a true four-beat walk, but the trot and canter must be collected and elevated." Royal Flush was showcased in a number of horse competitions and earned prizes for her owner (Nellie). An expert equestrian, Nellie Green was considered one of the finest horseback riders in Connecticut.

3

TRAGEDY STRIKES

Sugar, Charlie's been drowned fishin' off Townsend Ledge
—Charles Green

In 1895, the first of several tragedies struck for Nellie Green. Charles Hinckley, born in October 1867, was a railroad engineer on the New Haven, New York and Hartford lines. Nellie was very fond of Hinckley, saying he was "as fine a man as God ever let live." After a brief courtship, Charles and Nellie were married. Nellie was seventeen years old. They were to be married for only four years.

On Wednesday October 23, 1895, Nellie left for Washington, D.C., for a singing engagement at the home of a wealthy and influential merchant. Nellie was in Washington when her father telegraphed her that Hinckley had been injured in an accident on Sunday, October 27, 1895. Nellie explained it this way:

> *When I returned home from Washington, Papa said to me in almost a whisper "Sugar, Charlie's been drowned fishin' off Townsend Ledge." I was in total shock. I knew Charlie could easily swim the "pond" (the lee stretch between Long Island and the mainland, 'bout 20 miles), so their skiff must 'ave turned over sudden like when a storm came up off Townsend Ledge. No one saw nawthin'. It was October 1895. Many's the night when the tide was comin' in, that I went out to Mansfield Grove, usually alone, and trudged along Cozy Beach, pokin' into the seaweed with*

Charles Hinckley at the helm of his train.

my arms looking for him, but found nawthin'. He was gone about five weeks when "a ducker" (hunter) found him on Thanksgiving Day, three o'clock in the afternoon on November 28, 1895—wedged between two rocks, three feet under the sea in the breakwater.

After hearing the details of her husband's drowning, Nellie felt a range of emotions—guilt, sadness, helplessness. She also felt an irony of fate knowing that she saved so many people from drowning in the whirlpool under the Farm River bridge, yet she was not there to save her own twenty-eight-year-old husband.

In addition to handling all the household finances and managing the Dyke House Inn, Nellie had to contend with the sudden loss of her husband, her father's severe mental condition and her mother's worsening eyesight and eventual blindness (which required Nellie's constant attention and worry). This all had a profound effect on Nellie. In her own words,

I became too tired to think straight. It even got to the point, so help me God, that I purchased some poison—enough to put my father, my mother, and myself away for good. It got that bad. But it was Mister Lynch, a very fine gent, the one who used to get my father's fightin' chickens from Ireland, who stepped in. When Mr. Lynch heard about it, he somehow talked me out of it.

Tragedy would strike again. This time it was her father. Charles Green's mental state became extremely unmanageable, to the point that Nellie feared that he would go out of the house at night and do harm to either someone else or to himself. She was terrified of this reality. As noted by Nellie's family members, the only way Nellie was able to ensure that Charles would not bolt out of the house was to tie a string to her wrist and his wrist and sleep on the floor beside him. Although her father was as strong as a bull, she always managed to control him. But he was a very tortured man, and even Nellie had to concede that she did as much as she could but he needed help beyond what she could provide. It finally got to the point where her father needed to be admitted to an asylum in Middletown, Connecticut.

Nellie always believed that her father's mental condition was due to the Minié ball that struck him in the forehead when he was a fifteen-year-old drummer boy in the Civil War. As Nellie put it, "The hole in his forehead was so big you can put your finger in it, and it must have done somethin' to his skull and caused a pressure on his brain all those years." Caring for her father was both mentally draining and financially challenging. Nellie had spent all her father's $10,000 in ready cash. In an effort to seek assistance to increase her father's $16 a month military pension, Nellie sought the advice of New Haven's John Addison Porter, who was a friend of the family. More importantly, Porter was President McKinley's secretary. Porter arranged for Nellie to meet personally with the president, which she recounted:

> *I went to the White House, I wasn't afraid, not a bit, and I saw President McKinley. After I've gone through the big rooms with the grand chandeliers, he received me on the first floor of his office in the back somewhere. He certainly was real nice. The President looked over all of Papa's papers from the Civil War, his discharge and such. He then tole me he'd attend to it. And he did. My father's pension was upped from 16 to 72 dollars a month—and that was a lot of money in those days. Only, my father didn't live long enough to enjoy it.*

Nellie's father was a dominant figure in Nellie's life. As she put it, "My father was the only one whoever dictated to me—the only one. My father was my boss. He said 'Sugar, I'd rather see you dead than see you become a bad woman. You remember that!' I never forget what he said."

There can be no dispute that Nellie's father was a flawed man. As noted in many media accounts, Charles was arrested on a number of occasions for breach of peace and other offenses throughout his life. In all likelihood, the injury he sustained as a boy during the war had a lifelong, devastating effect on his physical and psychological well-being. It also helps explain his violent tendencies and Nellie's unusual upbringing. But in his own way, he did show considerable love for his family, especially for his daughter, Sugar. And many of his neighbors saw a heroic and compassionate side. Take for instance the courage and compassion he showed in saving the lives of several of his East Haven neighbors. Media accounts have noted heroic actions, including a rescue that occurred in 1880. This particular incident occurred on Saturday, July 17, 1880. An East Haven resident by the name of Humphrey Holden was sailing his skiff along Farm River when his boat hit a portion of the Farm River bridge, and as a result, he fell overboard. Holden faced certain death as he was caught up in the strong current and the whirlpool under the bridge. His cries for help were heard by Charles Green, who jumped into his boat and rescued Holden by pulling him out of the water and into his boat. Charles, who was thirty-five years old at the time, risked his own life to save Holden from drowning under the Farm River bridge.

Charles Green died in November 1898. The funeral was held at the Dyke House at 2:30 p.m. on Friday, November 17, 1898, officiated by Reverend Dr Lines. Nellie was twenty-five years old.

William Barnes Talmadge.

The death of her father in November 1898 freed Nellie of the shackles of a man she both feared and respected. Her father's passing was in many ways a welcome relief for Nellie, since she no longer had to face such a violent person again in her life. And so, on May 17, 1900, the twenty-six-year-old Nellie married her childhood sweetheart, William Barnes Talmadge. Nellie said of Talmadge, "He was a good, decent man. Talmadge was a carpenter, a mechanic, a boat builder—you name it. He could do anythin' with his hands." The marriage took place in St. Paul's Church in New Haven. Nellie was happy again.

As noted by the Talmadge-Green family, William was a descendant of the famed Benjamin Tallmadge, aide-de-camp to General George Washington. Benjamin

Young Charlie (Nellie's son).

was also the leader of the famed Culper Spy Ring against the British during the American Revolutionary War. William Tallmadge's ancestors were some of the first settlers of New Haven, Connecticut.

The third major tragedy in Nellie's life (and the most devastating) was dealing with her son Charlie's illness and death. This tragedy would take its toll on Nellie both emotionally and financially.

Nellie's son, born on Saturday, September 14, 1901, was named Charles William Green Talmadge. Nellie provided the rationale behind her son's full name: "I gave him those names because I knew there'd never be another." Nellie always called him Charlie. Coincidentally, Charlie was born on the same day that President McKinley (who was of personal help to Nellie and her father) died after having been shot in Buffalo, New York, eight days earlier.

Charlie attended Hopkins School in New Haven. Hopkins is a private college-preparatory, coed school. Charlie was a bright, charming young man who showed a great deal of promise to achieve his goal to become a lawyer. He graduated from Hopkins before he was sixteen. Charlie was accepted into Colgate University (Hamilton, New York), where he intended to prepare for a degree in corporation law. After Colgate, his intention was to attend Harvard University. Once he became a lawyer, Charlie's goal was to leave East Haven and settle in Pennsylvania.

Nellie was very proud of her son:

> Becomin' a lawyer, that was his idea. He was always hangin' around with lawyers and judges—men old enough to be his father. They were big shots in New Haven, and they took quite an interest in my Charlie. They saw a future in him. That boy would sit in at all the important trials, like as if he was already a judge, and drink in the evidence and figure things out himself for himself. He didn't care much for criminal cases. He didn't like anythin' cheap or sensational. He was clean all the way through. The head man in the legal Department of the Pennsylvania Railroad Company met my Charlie here and he wanted him to work as an understudy or somethin'.

Charlie at Hopkins college-preparatory school (New Haven).

Nellie continued,

> *So, we planned that Charlie would go to Colgate, which he wished to because his professors at Hopkins had come from there and he thought they was fine teachers, as indeed they were. And then he would go to Harvard for his law work. He didn't want to go to Yale—not that he didn't respect the college but that it was too close to Farm River. He was always talkin' about Harvard. To my mind, he was talkin' as much about escapin' from the River and what it all stood for to him. And I understood, yes, indeed I did. My, but he was a serious-minded boy. But he did pretty much all the things kids do. He was always playin' tricks, he was always up to pranks. He was chock full of fun. Boys who wanted to get out of trouble used to come to my Charlie and talk their problems out with him. He always seemed so much older than the kids his own age. He could laugh, all right, never you fear, but he was a thinker, he was grave in his mind, and he had more than his fair share of the milk of human kindness. When I seen all this goin' on I said to myself, my Charlie is a-goin' to amount to somethin'. And when he does, he, Will, and I are going to sell all our properties here and move far away from Farm River.*

Nellie spared no expense on making sure Charlie had all the luxuries that she didn't have growing up:

> *He had more boats than he could use on the River, and an automobile of his own—which few boys of his age had at the time. And we made sure Charlie had all the money he needed—although he was sparin' of its use, he was always responsible. We also fixed up his room upstairs at the Hotel to make it as private and comfortable as possible. With our permission, Charlie loved steerin' one of my boats (the* Onward*) when the men took her out for a casual sail. He wasn't lackin' in nawthin', but he wasn't spoiled either, and that's what we wanted, Will and I. We watched him and never had no fears about that.*

Nellie would always be sure to instill in Charlie many life lessons. She gave him a number of tasks so he could learn both business skills and people skills:

> *Come Monday mornin's, I always had a lot of bills to pay, and I was always particular about payin' them on time. And I had a lot of money in the bank. So, I'd give Charlie as much as $1,000 at a time, often more,*

Charlie Talmadge taking his turn behind the wheel on one of Nellie's vessels.

and I'd send him into town to take care of my business. I'd tell him, "Son, you look out for strangers when you're walking on the streets, especially Commerce Street, with all that money. You watch out if any stranger comes up to you. But if you see a man lyin' in some gutter, drunk, maybe you stop and stir him up and find out who he is and if he needs anythin'. You can bet your boots, son, when you see a man in that condition, he's a-runnin' away from sump'n, perhaps from bad news at home. Who knows from what? That's why men drink to forget—the damn fools! But don't give him enough money to start drinkin' again, jest you see that he has a cup of coffee, or some breakfast to put in his belly in order, and car fare to go home where he belongs—and you do the same thing for any lady, especially any lady with a baby, if she's in trouble. And if you can't manage it for some reason, then just call me. I'll come a-runnin' to help, you can count on that!"

With his mother's loving guidance, Charlie learned how to take care of people in need and to take care of himself. It came natural to him. As Nellie said, "It wasn't that I taught him so much as he wanted to do it himself, on his own account, in his own right, and without talkin' about it. He was kind, he was interested, he was well educated, and he didn't pass judgement on nobody. Maybe that's one reason he was so keen on law."

In July 1916, Charlie began to experience very serious medical problems. They would soon become life-altering for Charlie—and for Nellie and Will.

On one hot day in July, Charlie tired himself out tugging rowboats into position in the water while he was swimming. He thought nothing of it and went to sleep at the usual time and with no problem. The following day was another hot summer day. So his father advised him to take the day off from working and cool off in the Farm River. Charlie took his father's advice and enjoyed his free day swimming in the river. When he got back to the hotel, Charlie began to experience terrible headaches. Seeing this, Nellie called the doctor and told Charlie to go lie down on his bed. Nellie explained what happened next: "While we was waitin' for the doctor to come, Charlie got up to go to the bathroom. And then I heard him laughin.' I said 'what's so funny son.' He said 'Oh mother nothin'—except I can't walk straight. I keep staggerin' as if I was drunk.'" Nellie then summoned a specialist who was a guest at the Hotel Talmadge. After a thorough examination, the specialist concluded that Charlie had infantile paralysis (polio). "So, I asked the doctor 'In God's name what is that?' The doctor explained and said that there's an awful lot of that goin' around. He tole me 'I hate to say it, I hope I'm wrong, but your boy acts as if he has it.'" That indeed is what he had.

Nellie recalled staying up all night staring at the Farm River through her bedroom window. She began to weep uncontrollably and angrily cursed the river. In her mind, Nellie's superstition about the Farm River was confirmed. Whether justified or not, she held the river responsible for the condition of her son. After all, her son was fine until he spent the past two days swimming in the Farm River.

The next day, Nellie made some calls and arranged to have Charlie seen by the finest doctors and receive the best treatment available—no matter what the cost. Nellie hired a well-known specialist to provide continual treatment for Charlie. In addition, she hired two nurses to care for her son on a daily basis. With each passing day, Nellie and Will became more panic-stricken. "We slept in snatches. Greatly loved was this lad." And in less than two weeks, the moment that Nellie and Will both had feared transpired

Early one morning when Will and I was catching a few winks, the nurse came in and said "Get up Mrs. Talmage and you Mr. Talmage the crisis is on." I said "Oh my God you mean Charlie is passing away?" She said

"I don't know, I've called the doctor and I hope not, but you'd better come right in." When Will and I ran in there my Charlie's head was jerkin' back. I spoke to him but at first, he couldn't answer me. He was pullin' his head back. I said to my Charlie "son you jest look straight at me, you look right at your mother and you keep lookin'. There ain't nawthin' the matter with you. Nawthin' at all. You're goin' to be alright. You jest keep lookin' straight at your mother." Pretty soon, he must have heard me, he opened his eyes and he looked at me and he said quiet-like "Yes mother there is. I'm havin' trouble with my neck." I told him never mind jest keep lookin' at me, and I tole' his father to be quiet, his neck was alright. Then he slumped over and Will cries out "Christ he's gone, he's dead." But he wasn't, thank God. It was jest that the crisis was over, and my Charlie was tired out. But he was paralyzed.

Her son was eventually transferred to a sanitarium in New Hampshire, "where he had the best of care."

After spending a year in New Hampshire, Charlie returned to live in the Hotel Talmadge. He now wore braces on both his legs. Knowing her

Charlie at a polio treatment facility in New Hampshire.

son might not (or would not) be able to return to school, Nellie hired two professors from Yale to help Charlie with his studies on a daily basis.

For nearly four years, Nellie steadfastly ensured that her son received the best support, whether at the sanitarium or at the Hotel Talmadge—both medical and academic support. Despite having difficulty walking, Charlie was able to drive his car and his father's large trucks.

Eventually, Charlie decided to forego his educational goals and go into his own business. Once again, Nellie knew just what to do. Charlie became the manager of the Ye Olde Bridge Beverage Company (also known as Olde Bridge Beverage Company). This was a bottling company that operated out of the converted stables in back of the hotel and became his mother's other enterprise. Nellie made it clear what Charlie's role would be during Prohibition: "Once Prohibition began, there was no connection—none—between Charlie's initial experiences dispursin' legitimate beer, and the beginnin' of the Eighteenth Amendment. When Prohibition became law, I made absolutely sure that Charlie distributed only soft-drinks or legitimate 'near-beer.'"

Despite his protests about his mother's bootlegging and his disdain for rum, Charlie did insist on helping his mother at critical times during Prohibition. For example, Charlie drove the car leading a caravan of liquor-laden trucks for rumrunners through Connecticut to drop off their illegal cargo on the border of Massachusetts. (Nellie charged rumrunners transportation fees of $2,500 per trip.)

Also, it was Charlie who volunteered to be a lookout at East Haven's Cow and Calf to give the all-clear sign for Nellie's rumrunners as they approached their destination at the Hotel Talmadge. (The Cow and Calf is a rock formation off the coast of East Haven in Long Island Sound at the mouth of Farm River.)

Furthermore, it was Charlie who agreed to be a decoy to throw off a state police pursuit when things got "hot" and Nellie needed to move her liquor cargo immediately out of the Hotel Talmadge.

While she appreciated the assistance she received in desperate times from both Charlie and her husband, Will, Nellie would still question their decisions to help out, feeling that they both should be "stayin' where they orter been in the first place if they had any brains."

On June 29, 1925, Charlie married Elizabeth "Betty" Cornelia Blackwell. The marriage took place in the main dining room of the Hotel Talmadge. There were well over five hundred guests in attendance. Celebrated harpist Edith Davis Jones (of Branford, Connecticut) played "Here Comes the Bride"

Right: Nellie Green and grandson Charles II (Charlie's son).

Below: Charles II (Charlie's son) standing next to his private airplane.

William II, Charlie's son (*right*), standing next to one of his two private airplanes at Madison's Griswold Airport.

as the couple walked down the aisle. Nellie performed "Oh Promise Me" for this happy wedding occasion. Much to the surprise of the wedding guests, Nellie closed the bar for the entire day. Nellie banned liquor from being served for this special occasion. The only exception was a mild champagne punch used for the wedding toast. No one dared suggest that the bar should be open—at least not to Nellie's face.

Charlie Talmage and his wife made the Hotel Talmadge their home. The hotel was, for a long while, also the home of their two children, Charles II and William II. Both of Charlie's sons were boat owners and had their own private airplanes. William II had two private airplanes, which he kept at the former Griswold Airport in Madison, Connecticut (next door to Young's Village). One was a white Piper Cub with red trim. He also rebuilt a silver fighter plane.

On October 6, 1942, with his father and mother, his wife and his two sons at his bedside, Charlie Talmage died of a cerebral hemorrhage. It was the beginning of his father William's gradual but progressive decline. For Nellie, it had a profound effect. Charlie's death would haunt her for the rest of her life.

4

NELLIE'S HEROICS AND THE BRIDGE

FARM RIVER HEROICS

I guess he didn't know how much the complete savin' of that horse would have meant to me—so much more than the diamond ring.

—Nellie Green

There were many sides of Nellie Green that many people admired—her courage, her substantial (but private) generosity and her willingness to help others, even if it meant putting her own life in peril. A perfect example is the fact that between the ages of sixteen and thirty, Nellie saved the lives of over twenty men, women and children whose rowboats and canoes overturned in the dangerous whirlpool that occurred at high tide in the Farm River. As Nellie recalled of one rescue:

At the time, a sudden and dangerous whirlpool would develop in the Farm River, at high tide, under the bridge with a rise of well over six feet, and rushin' through the gates on the north side. It was a dangerous trap, especially if you didn't see it a-comin. One day, my father and I was a-sittin' on the porch, I just turned sixteen, and Mr. Smedley (of the Smedley company) and his wife were headed east across the bridge to Branford, in their fancy horse wagon drivin by Mr. Warren (president of the New Haven Horse Railroad Company). For some reason, the horse rear'd in the air and threw his front feet over the rock wall of the bridge, and got 'em tangled up in the harness, and then he started a-kickin'. While my father was holdin' the carriage back to save the old folks (they were lyin' underneath it on the bridge), I took his knife and cut the traces and let the horse go overboard into the whirlpool, as in his panic he seemed determined to do. God knows, there wasn't any other place he could go, poor devil.

It was then that Nellie risked her own life to try to save this horse that was sure to drown:

The whirlpool turned the horse over and over, and when he'd gone around twice—he was drownin'. So, I took off my shoes and jumped off the bridge and onto his back. My father yelled at me, "Sugar, you God damned fool, let him go! There ain't nawthin' you can do for him—he's gone—he'll drown!" But I didn't pay no attention to my father and the others. As the whirlpool was sweepin' him, over and over, I jump'd on his back and cut the check-rein, and his head comes right up, and he was breathin' right, and he started swimmin' the way the whirlpool wanted him to go. I yelled for a rope. George Prout of Short Beach threw one down to me. The first time I missed, but the second time I didn't. Then, hitchin' him, I slipped off and swam ashore, and they led him in. However, comin' up the slippery rocks the horse cut an artery and he slashed his legs a-beatin' 'em on the rocks of the bridge wall, and he was bleedin' badly. So we called "Doc" Whitney—he was a vet in New Haven—and he came rushin' out, and he shot him. He put him away. That horse—a beautiful chestnut, sixteen-hand horse—cost more than $1,500. And so, I managed to save the horse from the river, but couldn't save him once he got all cut up. Mr. Warren, he was grateful for what I'd done, said I'd never have to look for a job if ever I had a need of one. He gave me a present of a beautiful diamond ring which I only took because he insisted so much. I guess he didn't know how much the complete savin' of that horse would have meant to me so much more than the diamond ring. Well, that's the kind of thing you can't very well explain.

Another rescue incident, involving a mayor and his family, is worth mentioning. Nellie recalled,

Mayor Frank Rice of New Haven was a very fine man. I knew him before he was mayor. One afternoon, the mayor, his uncle, and his cousin came down the river, and they went through the dykes [sic], and they struck the

gates and that turned all three of 'em bottom side up. When I saw what was a-happenin' I jumped into my rowboat and I saw the uncle go down and when he come up (of course, he would've gone down again), I got him by the shoulders and he very near pulled me out of my boat. So, I had to lay down and put my feet against the sides, bracin' the both of us, to hold on to him. People began hollerin'. Then the current took us, the boat and him and me, to where it would get shallow, to where his feet would strike the clam bed, and he could get a footin'. So, when that happened, I hauled him in my boat and rowed him ashore, and the old gent was exhausted. The mayor, he was hangin' on the gates and he was a-flappin'. So, I fetched him also. The mayor, his uncle, and his cousin were a-puffin but they all heaved a sigh of relief. And so, it had a happy ending. Mayor Rice wanted to pay me but I said no, I was only too glad to be on hand to help. He tole me that if he could ever do me a favor he would always be willing to help me out, or if I was ever in trouble to come and see him. I thanked him but I told the mayor I don't do things like that for no favors. I was jest glad I was able to save all of them.

And so, it was her compassion and unselfish actions in situations like this that won the hearts of so many of the people around town for Nellie Green. When Prohibition came around, people from surrounding towns all supported Nellie, knowing how much she had done for the community.

The river under the Farm River bridge was known to rise well over six feet, causing a whirlpool effect.

The Bridge

And so, the tide comes in and the big barge goes up—and it took more than half the bridge with it. Honest to God, I thought I'd split my sides laughin'!

The owner of Trap Rock Quarry had a problem. His barges were having difficulty crossing under the Farm River timber drawbridge, which was having a negative effect on his quarry business. In order to raise the drawbridge, Nellie had to use a special long pole once she received a signal from the approaching barge. This had been Sugar's job ever since she was very young. It was a time-consuming and labor-intensive process. The quarry's owner pleaded with town officials in both East Haven and Branford to construct a new bridge over the Farm River, to no avail. The officials were adamant that there was no need for a new bridge. As a last resort, the quarry owner approached Nellie Green for her help in this matter. It was then that Nellie cooked up a scheme to ensure that the old bridge would have to be replaced.

Nellie instructed the quarry owner to tow a big barge and anchor it under the bridge at low tide. She related the rest of the story:

We had the crew of the barge come into the Dyke House Inn for refreshments. Seein' that no one was payin' attention to the barge under the bridge, I went out all friendly-like and got all the constables to also come into Dyke House Inn and made sure they were all oiled-up. They were frequent guests at the house and liked the likker we served, so no one suspected nawthin'. All the time I was keepin' an eye on the incomin' tide and the sudden whirlpool effect that would occur under the bridge at high tide. The officials were in no shape to watch the tide, much less think about it. And so, the tide comes in and the big barge goes up—and it took more than half the bridge with it! And then the barge went upstream about its business—with the bridge on it. The constables, they were all drunk and didn't know nawthin' about it. Honest to God, I thought I'd split my sides laughin'! And so, the quarry man got his new fancy bridge. No one ever knew I had a hand in all of this. Of course, there was hell to pay in the mornin' when the folks started drivin' in on their horse-drawn buggies from Branford or wherever and they couldn't go no place because there was no bridge. But that was up to the town officials to explain.

Nellie justified her actions with regards to the destruction of the bridge this way: "The quarry owner helped me out a good deal in the past, so why

Top: Older version of the Farm River Bridge with its wooden railings.

Middle: Old Farm River bridge destroyed (as planned by Nellie Green).

Bottom: The new reconstructed Farm River Bridge.

Nellie sporting a new coat (husband William standing).

wouldn't I help him this time? The town officials were not being fair and had no business refusin' to build a new bridge when it was sorely needed, and would help many of the town folks." With the entire bridge destroyed, it obviously inconvenienced the horse-drawn commuters. However, in the long run, building the new bridge proved to be a pleasant experience for the public. And of course, the new bridge was a blessing for the barges, as crossing under the Farm River bridge became much easier—thanks to Nellie Green.

Soon after this incident, Nellie was able to build a bridge of her own. As mentioned previously, after the deaths of her first husband and her father, she married her childhood sweetheart, William Barnes Talmadge.

5

THE PROHIBITION ACT

A great social and economic experiment, noble in motive
—Herbert Hoover, thirty-first president of the United States

A t midnight on Saturday January 17, 1920, the United States went dry. On that day and time, the Prohibition Act took effect, banning the "manufacture, sale, and distribution" of intoxicating liquor. Because of this law, saloons, distilleries and most breweries were forced to close their doors.

From its onset, the Prohibition era has intrigued Americans in a number of different ways. Some advocated for a national Prohibition law to curb the negative effects of alcohol abuse, believing it had a devastating effect on the family, especially wives and children. Others have felt (and still feel) that the Roaring Twenties was an exciting, glamorous, spirited time that brought about the independent "new woman." Still others felt that the Prohibition law was unjust and counterproductive—restricting a freedom they loved and enjoyed—and costly on a financial level.

So, how did we get to this historic and controversial moment in American history? Let's look back at the circumstances surrounding the Prohibition Act, mainly the temperance movement, the enforcement of the Volstead Act and the repeal of Prohibition.

Well over one hundred years before the Prohibition Act took effect, organized groups throughout the United States began their pursuit to limit or outlaw the consumption and production of alcoholic beverages. Purportedly, the first temperance group on record in the United States was formed in Litchfield County, Connecticut, in 1789.

Last call. Crowds rush to purchase liquor before the Prohibition law took effect. *Walter P. Reuther Library, Archives of Labor and Urban Affairs, Wayne State University.*

These organizations began to champion the cause for temperance, arguing that alcohol abuse was morally corrupting and destroying families—both personally and economically. This organized effort demanding restrictions on alcohol became known as the temperance movement.

The Temperance Movement (The "Drys")

I am the sworn, eternal and uncompromising enemy of the liquor traffic.
—Billy Sunday, famed orator

Proponents of the temperance movement viewed alcohol as a moral societal problem. It was their belief that alcohol affected not only the current society but future generations as well. Alcoholism, in their view, was the cause of "secondary poverty." To defend their position, temperance proponents cited numerous examples of alcoholic husbands wasting money on liquor, causing their families to fall below the poverty line. Proponents viewed alcohol as a form of oppression. They felt that the only solution to improve the lives of women and children and to make families stronger was through alcohol abstinence. Women in particular were drawn to the temperance movement in large numbers. Suffragists and their supporters aligned themselves with the temperance movement because they felt their causes were, in many ways, connected.

The nineteenth and early twentieth centuries saw a proliferation of temperance societies. The most noteworthy of these were the Woman's Christian Temperance Union (WCTU) and the American Anti-Saloon League (ASL). The Anti-Saloon League proved to be the most effective group in the pursuit of Prohibition because members applied effective political pressure to achieve their goals.

Proponents of temperance and Prohibition were known as the "drys," while those opposed came to be known as the "wets."

Here are several examples of prominent drys.

Susan B. Anthony

Noted suffragist Susan B. Anthony, whose father was a temperance advocate, became actively involved in the movement at an early age. In fact, her first public speech was on the subject of temperance on March 2, 1849, when she addressed two hundred women of the Daughters of Temperance. She spoke with determination and courage; at the time, it was not common for women to speak in public, much less on matters such as this. At the time, Anthony was a twenty-nine-year-old headmistress of the girls' department at Canajoharie Academy (New York). She was also the presiding sister of the Daughters of Temperance, whose motto was "Virtue, Love, and Temperance."

In her speech, Anthony advocated for discontinuing sales of intoxicating liquor in communities to influence male behavior. Susan B. Anthony viewed temperance as a women's issue, as, in her opinion, alcohol abuse was detrimental to the lives of women and children.

Anthony was also a staunch advocate of women's right to vote. Just seven months after the passage of the Prohibition Act, the Nineteenth Amendment was enacted, granting women the right to vote.

Frances Willard

Temperance is the moderation of things that are good and the total abstinence from the things that are foul.

—Frances Willard

Frances Willard was the national president of the Woman's Christian Temperance Union (WCTU) from 1879 to 1898. She was a staunch temperance advocate and suffragist. Willard's advocacy was influential in the passage of the Eighteenth and Nineteenth Amendments to the U.S. Constitution.

Wayne Wheeler

As the leader of the Anti-Saloon league, Wayne Wheeler was extremely instrumental in the passage of the Eighteenth Amendment. The wets coined the term *Wheelerism* to refer to Wheeler's persuasive—some would say threatening—tactics to get politicians to agree with the principles of the Prohibition movement.

Marie C. Brehm

Marie C. Brehm was a staunch advocate of Prohibition, a suffragist and a politician. In 1924, Brehm (of California) became the first female candidate to run for the vice presidency of the United States (on the Prohibition Party ticket) after women were allowed to vote in a national election. This enabled Brehm to vote for herself in the election. At the invitation of Connecticut temperance crusader Emil L.G. Hohenthal, Brehm campaigned in Hartford, Connecticut, in September 1924.

Carrie A. Nation

Men are nicotine-soaked, beer-besmirched, whiskey-greased, red-eyed devils.

—Carrie Nation

Carrie (Carry) Amelia Nation was a controversial anti-alcohol advocate. She became famous (or infamous) due to her extreme and, at times violent,

Carrie Nation. *Special Collections & University Archives, Pittsburg State University, Pittsburg, Kansas.*

opposition of alcohol, such as destroying bars, saloons and pharmacies with a hatchet. Nation referred to these attacks as "hatchetations," for which she was arrested numerous times. At other times, she would use rocks (which she called "smashers") as her weapon and would proceed to smash all the liquor bottles in one saloon after another. She once proudly stated, "I felt invincible. My strength was that of a giant. I smashed five saloons with rocks before I ever took a hatchet." Her actions were not condoned by many other temperance advocates.

She changed her first name to Carry, saying her name meant "Carry A Nation for Prohibition." Quite an interesting historical character, to say the least.

Billy Sunday

As Billy Sunday was a powerful orator and a strong supporter of temperance and Prohibition, his influential preaching about the evils of alcohol helped sway public opinion in favor of the Eighteenth Amendment. At one point during a crusade in Boston, Sunday exclaimed, "Whiskey and beer are all right in their place, but their place is in hell."

Connecticut's Role in the Temperance Movement

There were a number of groups and individuals from the state who were actively involved in the temperance movement. Here are just of few of the Connecticut organizations and individuals that favored temperance.

◊ Litchfield County | Allegedly, the first temperance society on record in the United States was formed in Litchfield County, Connecticut, in 1789.

◊ The Connecticut Society for the Reformation of Morals | The Connecticut Society for the Reformation of Morals was an anti-liquor organization founded in 1813. The organization was led by Protestant ministers who emphasized the "sin" of overindulging in alcohol. The group did not call for the elimination of drinking altogether but rather a more restrained approach to drinking alcoholic beverages.

◊ Lyman Beecher | In 1826, Lyman Beecher of New Haven, Connecticut, published a book called *Six Sermons on Intemperance* in which he described alcohol abuse (intemperance) as a "national sin." Beecher favored legislation to prohibit the sales of alcohol.

◊ Irving Fisher | Noted economist Irving Fisher was a strong promoter of Prohibition. After receiving a doctorate from Yale University (New Haven), he later became a professor of political economy at Yale. While at Yale, he was also a member of the secretive Skull and Bones Society. Fisher was an advocate for the legal prohibition of alcohol and wrote three publications defending Prohibition, citing the negative effect that alcohol had on public health and U.S. productivity.

◊ Betsy M. Parsons | Hartford, Connecticut native Betsy M. Parsons was a stanch proponent of the temperance movement. Parsons was one of the leaders of the women's suffrage crusade in Connecticut. She was instrumental in arranging for the suffrage convention held in the Hartford Opera House in 1869. Speakers at the 1869 Hartford Convention included prominent temperance advocates Elizabeth Cady Stanton, Susan B. Anthony, William Lloyd Garrison and Henry Ward Beecher. Beecher was a native of Litchfield, Connecticut, and the brother of Harriet Beecher Stowe, who was also a Litchfield resident. As a result of that convention, the Connecticut Women Suffrage Association was formed, and Betsy Parsons was a founding officer of that organization.

◊ THE CONNECTICUT TEMPERANCE SOCIETY | On May 20, 1829, the Connecticut Temperance Society became affiliated with the American Temperance Society. Included in its ranks was the influential crusader Reverend Lyman Beecher, father of Harriet Beecher Stowe and Henry Ward Beecher.

◊ THE CONNECTICUT TEMPERANCE UNION | The Connecticut Temperance Union (CTU), founded in 1865, was the state representative of the powerful national Anti-Saloon League. Kensington, Connecticut native H.H. Spooner served as the secretary of the CTU. Spooner often warned of the "Curse of the Saloon," stating that the saloon, tavern or bar was an "undesirable feature in any community."

EMIL L.G. HOHENTHAL

Beware of the Siren of the Deceiver
—Emil L.G. Hohenthal

One of the staunchest supporters of the Prohibition movement was Emil Louis George Hohenthal of Manchester, Connecticut. Hohenthal was a prominent member of a national temperance organization and an internationally known crusader for Prohibition. Hohenthal represented Connecticut in numerous Prohibition activities both within the state and throughout the world.

In 1887, Hohenthal joined the local Sons of Temperance organization in New Haven, Connecticut. Later, he was chosen to become a member of the National Sons of Temperance organization in New York, where he served as a high-ranking officer within the organization. Hohenthal eventually retired from his contracting business in Manchester to concentrate on his advocacy and the Sons of Temperance organization.

As a staunch crusader for the Prohibition cause, Hohenthal advocated for "total abstinence," saying that the Prohibition Act was not stringent enough since it allowed for one half of 1 percent of alcohol in beverages.

Emil L.G. Hohenthal. *Author's collection*.

In a 1918 keynote speech at a Prohibition Party governor's convention in Hartford, Connecticut, Hohenthal warned of an effort by the wets to mislead people into some sort of compromise on the trafficking of liquor: "Today the Prohibition Party sounds the warning to the vast number of optimistic recruits to the Prohibition cause not to be carried away by the siren of the deceiver."

Hohenthal was an advocate of restrictive liquor laws for forty-six years. He had thousands of supporters throughout Connecticut. However, this was not enough for Hohenthal to win any of the major political campaigns in which he was involved. In 1920, Hohenthal was a candidate on the Prohibition ticket for U.S. Senate, with a temperate campaign slogan: "the only dry candidate." He also ran for the U.S. House of Representatives (1898) and governor (1910). He was defeated soundly in all three campaigns.

Hohenthal was a delegate from Connecticut to the International Anti-Alcohol Congress in Washington, D.C., in 1920. He was even appointed by President Harding as one of the U.S. delegates to an Anti-Alcohol Congress in Lausanne, Switzerland, in 1921.

Between 1922 and 1927, Hohenthal toured Europe four times to promote Prohibition organizations. He was European secretary of the International Reform Federation. He was also the European director of the World Prohibition Federation.

Emil L.G. Hohenthal died suddenly of a heart attack on a train en route to St. Louis. His son, Louis Lester Hohenthal, succeeded Emil in his role with the Sons of Temperance organization.

NATIONAL PROHIBITION BEGINS

During Prohibition it was said tailors would ask customers what size pockets they wanted, pint or quart.

—Will Rogers

In 1919, while Americans were being entertained by such classic songs as "After You've Gone" by Marion Harris and movies such as the top-grossing *The Miracle Man*, Congress was about to enact the historic and controversial Prohibition Act later that same year.

As was previously noted, organizations such as the Anti-Saloon League had a profound effect on many Americans and politicians who demanded

Moments before Prohibition took effect. *Library of Congress.*

swift action on the restriction of liquor sales in the United States. In their minds, the time to act was now.

So here, in brief, were the actions taken by Congress (and the president).

In 1917, the chairman of the House Judiciary Committee introduced language of the Eighteenth Amendment for adoption by Congress. The chairman's name was Andrew J. Volstead, and he became known as the "Father of Prohibition." The legislation was highly influenced by Wayne Wheeler of the Anti-Saloon League, who purportedly conceived and wrote most of the amendment language. Volstead was a lifelong teetotaler and was mocked by the wets movement as the "Wet Blanket."

Advocates on both sides of the alcohol campaign were fully aware of the distinction between the temperance movement and the more controversial prohibition movement. They understood that temperance usually referred to moderate liquor use or abstinence from drinking liquor, mainly on a voluntary basis. On the other hand, national Prohibition would make it illegal to manufacture, sell, or transport alcohol.

Led by the organized efforts of the temperance movement and the Anti-Saloon League, the Eighteenth Amendment passed both the U.S. House of Representatives and the Senate. However, President Woodrow Wilson vetoed the legislation. By a two-thirds majority, Congress overrode the president's veto, and the amendment was ratified on January 16, 1919, by the requisite three-fourths of the states. In all, forty-six of the forty-eight U.S. states ratified the Prohibition amendment. Interestingly, Connecticut was only one of two states that refused to ratify the amendment. (The other state was Rhode Island.) On February 4, 1919, by a vote of 20–14, the Connecticut Senate declined to ratify the Eighteenth Amendment.

And so, the stage was set for the enaction of national Prohibition, commonly referred to as the Volstead Act, which passed on October 28, 1919. U.S. undersecretary of state Frank L. Lyon announced on January 16, 1919, that the amendment had been ratified and would go into effect in exactly one year (January 17, 1920). The National Prohibition Act banned the "manufacture, sale and transportation of intoxicating liquors"

Volstead's reign as the Father of Prohibition was short-lived, however, as he was defeated in the 1922 congressional primary by the walrus mustachioed Ole J. Kvale. During the primary campaign, Kvale implied, without outright saying, that Volstead was an atheist who was opposed to the Bible. The implication was enough for many voters to turn against Volstead.

The Eighteenth Amendment banned the "manufacture, sale and transportation of intoxicating liquors"—but not the actual consumption of alcohol. People were allowed to drink in their own homes, assuming they were not in the bootlegging business. Many historians believe that the term *bootlegging* originated during the American Civil War, when soldiers would smuggle liquor into army camps by concealing pint bottles of alcohol inside their boots or within their trouser legs.

The Prohibition Act established the legal definition of intoxicating liquors as well as penalties for producing them. The legal definition of illegal liquor was "alcohol of no more than 0.5 percent alcohol content."

Herbert Hoover

I do not favor the repeal of the Eighteenth Amendment
—Herbert Hoover, thirty-first president

As a Presidential candidate in 1928, Herbert Hoover pledged his support of the Eighteenth Amendment, calling Prohibition "a great social and economic experiment, noble in motive."

Jeanette Rankin. *Library of Congress*.

Jeanette Rankin

Jeanette Rankin (Montana congresswoman) voted for the Eighteenth Amendment. At the time, Rankin was the first—and at that time, only—woman in Congress.

The National Prohibition Party

In 1869, the National Prohibition Party was formed as a third political party. The main reason for the creation of the Prohibition Party was because some Americans felt that the existing Democrat and Republican Parties did not do enough for the temperance cause.

In the late 1800s, the National Prohibition Party nominated candidates in each presidential election. All were unsuccessful and roundly defeated by the Republican or Democratic candidates. The first National Prohibition Party presidential candidate was James Black (Pennsylvania), nominated in 1872. The last Prohibition Party candidate for president was William David Upshaw (Georgia) in 1932.

Flaunting the Prohibition Act

Tomorrow we may die, so let's get drunk and make love.
—*Lipstick (a.k.a. Lois Long)*

For many people during the Prohibition era, alcohol became a symbol of independence, sophistication, romance and adventure. In numerous towns across the United States, including Westport, Connecticut, people openly flaunted the Eighteenth Amendment, knowing that local law enforcement could not or would not properly enforce the Prohibition law. Speakeasies and bootleggers alike satisfied Americans' high demand for illegal liquor throughout much of the United States. Women, as well as men, were actively involved in the consumption and sale of illegal alcohol. During the course of Prohibition, American sentiment shifted dramatically and in increasing numbers toward the repeal of the Prohibition Act.

Flappers at a speakeasy bar. *Author's collection.*

Flaunting the Prohibition Act. *Author's collection.*

We women had been emancipated and we weren't sure what we were supposed to do with all the freedom and equal rights, so we were going to hell laughing and singing.

—*Lois Long*

PROHIBITION LOOPHOLES AND SNEAKY, CLEVER TRICKS

When my position was "hot" I would hide the booze on my premises in fake walls that nobody knew about.

—*Nellie Green, bootlegger*

While illegal alcohol was strictly defined by the Prohibition Act, several loopholes were allowed under the law, including doctors' prescriptions for medicinal whiskey. Also, the sale of near-beer (with very low alcohol content) was permitted under the Volstead Act. Despite the strict regulations on the sale of real alcohol, bootleggers and average citizens devised clever tricks and ways to circumvent the Prohibition Act. Here are a few.

Medicinal Whiskey

Drugstores were allowed to sell medicinal whiskey to treat everything from mouth sores to the common cold. Licensed physicians were allowed to write a prescription for one quart of whiskey per patient per month. Nearly everyone could get a prescription for a two-dollar office call fee. Thus, "patients" with an easily obtainable physician's prescription could legally buy a pint of hard liquor every ten days. And of course, some prescriptions were forgeries. As you can probably guess, many people took advantage of this loophole. During Prohibition, thousands of false prescriptions with doctors' names forged were uncovered.

Some breweries remained open despite the Prohibition ban. So how were they allowed to stay open? The answer is near-beer (sometimes called "cereal beverage"). The catch was that the breweries needed to first make real beer and then draw off alcohol until the beer reached the legal percentage of alcohol (i.e., no more than 0.5 percent alcohol content). Not surprisingly, in some instances, that second step was often left out. Prohibition agents could do nothing as long as it remained in the brewery

Doctor's prescription for "Medicinal Whiskey." *Author's collection.*

since breweries claimed it was awaiting the final step. Then, when the Prohibition agents were gone, trucks drove out carrying the real beer.

Cruises to Nowhere

Cruises to nowhere (a.k.a. "booze cruises") were an industry that became popular as a result of Prohibition. Ships would sail out to international waters, where they could legally serve alcohol, and the ship would typically cruise in circles. Cruises to nowhere were also a forerunner of the luxury cruise business. Prior to this time, people used ships for direct travel to specific destinations.

Rumrunner Trick

After picking up their cargo from Rum Row, many astute rumrunners would try to time their speedy dash to the shore when they knew that there would be a tow of barges heading down the coast. This would be an ideal situation for the rumrunner. A tow such as this would extend behind the tug for three hundred yards. The thick rope cables between the barges hung in the water at a depth of three feet or so. The rumrunner speedboats would easily zoom over the lines. Meanwhile, if Coast Guard boats attempted to follow, they would ram into the ropes. Other patrol boats would take the long way around the tow, enabling the rumrunners to gleefully escape.

Other clever tricks included:

◊ fake walls in speakeasies (one of the clever tricks used by Nellie Green)
◊ false floorboards in automobiles
◊ second gas tanks
◊ an underwater cable liquor delivery system (created by bootleggers)
◊ tin can "food"
◊ cartons of eggs with blown-out eggs filled with whiskey
◊ life preservers filled with liquor containers
◊ hidden flasks (common trick and a favorite among young women)
◊ walking canes

Flapper with hidden garter liquor flask. *Author's collection.*

◊ cow shoes (to throw off law enforcement agents during a chase,
   specially designed footprints in the shape of cow hooves were
   used by some bootleggers)

Above: Woman seated at a soda fountain table pours alcohol into a cup from a cane, 1922. *Library of Congress*.

Opposite: "Cow shoes" used by bootleggers in the 1920s Prohibition era. *Library of Congress*.

THE MAN IN THE GREEN HAT

In case you thought that members of Congress were not directly involved in activities involving illegal alcohol, consider the case of the "Man in the Green Hat."

In turns out that many congressmen actually had their own personal bootlegger by the name of George L. Cassiday. From 1920 to 1930, Cassiday supplied the members of both the House and the Senate with illegal booze. He would show up each day carrying a liquor-filled suitcase and wearing his trademark green fedora. He became such a welcoming figure that he was furnished office space across the street from the Capitol in the basement of the House Office Building (Cannon building). Members of Congress would gain entry into Cassiday's "office" by using a secret door knock. The lawmakers would drink and play cards in Cassiday's office while waiting for floor votes.

Cassiday was arrested by Capitol Police in 1925, when he was dealing mainly with House members. He then decided to shift his bootlegging activities to the Senate side since he found senators to be more discreet. However, Cassidy was arrested again in 1930 in a sting operation conducted by an undercover Prohibition Bureau agent named Roger Butts, who was

George L. Cassiday (and his hat). *Author's collection.*

referred to as the "dry spy." For this arrest, the bootlegger was sentenced to an eighteen-month prison term. Cassiday claimed that he supplied liquor to four out of five representatives and senators during the time that he was their bootlegger. George L. Cassiday became known as the "Man in the Green Hat."

ENFORCEMENT OF PROHIBITION

Dere's sad news here. You're under arrest.
—*Izzy Einstein, Prohibition agent*

The Eighteenth Amendment laid the groundwork for a bureau of federal agents to enforce the Prohibition Act. Enforcement of Prohibition was originally assigned to the Internal Revenue Service (IRS), a division of the Treasury Department. Thus, the Prohibition enforcement agents were called "revenuers." Following a realignment in the Prohibition Unit, anti-Prohibitionists referred to the enforcement agents as "prohis."

Initially, Prohibitionists (the drys) believed that the Volstead Act would be rather easy to enforce. It was their belief that the wets would gracefully accept the inevitability of Prohibition and obey the law that was just enacted.

At the beginning of Prohibition, Congress agreed with the drys that enforcement of the Volstead Act would not be difficult and counted on enforcement being inexpensive. To emphasize this point, the first Prohibition commissioner, John F. Kramer, boldly claimed, "This law will be obeyed in cities large and small without need of much intervention." Kramer noted that the Volstead Act's severe penalties of a fine of up to $1,000 and imprisonment of up to six months for the first offense would be a major deterrent to every American. (Later, the penalties for first-time offenders of the Volstead Act increased to a $10,000 fine and five years in prison.) Andrew Mellon was appointed as the treasury secretary and served from 1921 to 1932. (On a trivia note: The Monopoly board game's man with the black top hat and tails and white mustache was allegedly modeled after Mellon.)

Andrew Mellon.
Author's collection.

Kramer formed the Prohibition Unit, which initially consisted of only about 1,500 agents who received very low salaries. Their meager pay made some agents susceptible to bribery and payoffs. Purportedly, some agents even agreed to be put on speakeasy payrolls by bootleggers so that these illegal establishments could operate without interruption. In 1927, the unit became an independent entity within the Department of the Treasury, changing its name from the Prohibition Unit to the Bureau of Prohibition. Enforcement was eventually transferred to the Justice Department in 1930.

But what about the rumrunning that was occurring on the open seas? How was that enforced? The responsibility of enforcing illegal rumrunning on the waterways rested mainly with the Coast Guard. The U.S. Coast Guard (USCG) was formally established on January 28, 1915, when President Woodrow Wilson signed the Act to Create the Coast Guard into law by merging the Life-Saving Service and the Revenue Cutter Service. Like the enforcement agents on land, the USCG was initially undermanned and underequipped to combat the extensive waterway trafficking of illegal liquor, especially in areas such as Rum Row. The USCG did expand from its modest beginnings into a full military service of the United States (with customs authority) during the 1920s and received a substantial increase in funding and manpower. The Coast Guard had some success in seizing many rumrunning boats. However, despite the USCG's best efforts, a tremendous amount of liquor continued to be smuggled into the United States up until the repeal of Prohibition.

Of course, enforcement of the Prohibition Act would be anything but easy. The drys and Congress underestimated the anti-Prohibition sentiment, and it increased substantially over the course of the Prohibition era. They also underestimated the huge demand for alcohol by average citizens, despite the threat of severe penalties. They also miscalculated the willingness of so many people to disobey (or simply ignore) the law.

ELIOT NESS AND "THE UNTOUCHABLES"

I did want Al Capone and every gangster in the city to realize that there were still a few law enforcement agents who couldn't be swerved from their duty.
                                    —*Eliot Ness, law enforcement agent*

Eliot Ness credentials. *Courtesy of Dan Mancinone, former special agent, IRS Criminal Investigation.*

Eliot Ness became famous as the leader of a group of law enforcement agents known as "The Untouchables." He was assigned as a special agent under the Bureau of Prohibition, U.S. Department of the Treasury.

Ness and the Untouchables gained national acclaim in their relentless pursuit of the gangster Al Capone. The media reported on their every move to clean up the corruption by numerous mobs, especially toward the latter part of the Prohibition era. The Untouchables earned their nickname after repeatedly refusing to take bribes or be intimidated by Chicago gangs. Americans came to the realization that Eliot Ness was an incorruptible law enforcement agent.

AL CAPONE

The establishment of the 1919 Prohibition Act and the resulting expansive rise in bootlegging eventually led to the development of organized crime in the United States. The prohibition era was racked by crime and violence as ruthless gangs were engaged in the illegal business of selling liquor. The most notorious gangster at the time, Al Capone, rose to prominence as a bootlegger in Chicago. Eventually, public sentiment demanded that law enforcement curb this organized lawlessness.

It was difficult for local law enforcement to obtain evidence against these racketeers because the gangsters directed others to act for them, thus avoiding exposure to prosecution which would cause their own apprehension. The gangsters' corrupt alliance with dishonest politicians and police also hindered local law enforcement agencies in stopping the bootlegging.

In 1919, the U.S. Treasury established the Intelligence Unit and appointed Elmer Irey as its Chief. At the time, Al Capone was the most notorious gangster-bootlegger in the country. As such, Capone was investigated by the Intelligence Unit. His conviction relating to his failure to pay and/or file his income taxes between 1925 and 1929 was the first decisive blow struck at organized crime and the bootlegging industry. The Intelligence Unit evolved into the IRS Criminal Investigation Division, which is the current investigative and law enforcement arm of the Internal Revenue Service.

—Dan Mancinone, former special agent, IRS Criminal Investigation

The most famous American gangster during the Prohibition era was crime boss Al Capone, also known as "Scarface." Born Alphonse Gabriel Capone, Scarface ruled nearly every aspect of Chicago's alcohol industry from 1925 to 1931.

In 1919, U.S. Treasury official Elmer Irey created a special unit to crack down on tax evaders. Irey's "T-Men" became a leading force against corrupt politicians and mob bosses. The unit's most important achievement was to put Chicago mob boss Al Capone behind bars.

In June 1931, Capone was indicted for twenty-two counts of federal income tax evasion, followed by a charge of conspiracy to violate Prohibition laws. On October 17, 1931, Capone was tried and found guilty. Al Capone was sentenced to eleven years in prison and $50,000 in fines. He first entered the Atlanta penitentiary but was later transferred to the infamous Alcatraz prison.

TWO PIONEER WOMEN PROHIBITION AGENTS

Women resort to all sorts of tricks, concealing metal containers in their clothing, etc. Their detection and arrest are far more difficult than that of male lawbreakers.

—Georgia Hopley, 1922

In 1922, Georgia Hopley became the first female Prohibition agent when she was sworn into the Washington, D.C. Prohibition Unit by President Warren Harding in 1922. Hopley was appointed the director of publicity for the Prohibition Unit, and her job was to strengthen public support for the enforcement of Prohibition. She would do this by traveling across the United States and speaking to various groups and organizations about Prohibition enforcement issues, always raising awareness of the increase of female bootleggers.

Georgia Hopley.
Library of Congress.

"Lady Hooch Hunter" Daisy Simpson. *National Archives.*

Known as the "Lady Hooch Hunter," Daisy Simpson was a colorful and sometimes controversial Prohibition agent in the 1920s. Simpson performed her law enforcement duties using a wide variety of disguises combined with skillful acting. She used unusual, and some would say unethical, tactics to

Prohibition agents dumping beer into a sewer after a raid. *Library of Congress*.

Prohibition agents break up a speakeasy saloon. *Author's collection*.

Internal Revenue chemist G.F. Beyer testing confiscated liquor, 1920. *Library of Congress*.

apprehend unsuspecting bootleggers. One of her favorite methods was to sneak into a speakeasy and then tell the bartender that she felt ill and needed to go outside to get some air. Once the sympathetic bartender came out to politely offer her a glass of brandy to make her feel better, Simpson would immediately arrest him for violating the Prohibition Act.

Daisy Simpson also used a number of aliases (Daisy Burke, B.B. Moore and others) during the course of her enforcement work. For a time in the early 1920s, the print media was fascinated with her and her work. An example of this was the "thick ankles" episode, which occurred in 1924. At the time, Simpson had sprained both of her ankles in the line of duty, which caused both to become swollen. An unidentified bootlegger jokingly said that it was easy to spot agent Simpson (even if disguised) because of her "thick ankles." Hearing this, Simpson became enraged, accusing the bootlegger of libel and vowing that the bootlegger would be brought to justice. Newspapers across the country were enamored of this story, which made the front-page headline in a number of newspapers. She was referred to in the media as the "Two-Gun Woman" seeking revenge against the unknown bootlegger. During her four-year career as a Prohibition agent, Simpson received both praise and strong criticism. Police captain Charles Goff called her "a terror to liquor sellers and a nemesis of the underworld." On the other hand, Daisy Simpson was reprimanded in federal court for setting traps to entice bootleggers and her alleged unethical methods in making arrests.

IZZY AND MOE—"EINSTEIN'S THEORY"

Barnum was right: People will always let you fool them if you go about it the right way

—Izzy Einstein, Prohibition agent

Isidor "Izzy" Einstein and Moe W. Smith were very successful Prohibition agents. The dynamic duo of Izzy and Moe were credited with the most arrests and convictions during the first four years of the Prohibition era. The two made over 4,900 arrests, with a 95 percent conviction rate. They also confiscated over five million bottles of liquor, worth over $15 million.

Izzy and Moe became a public sensation and were the darlings of the media. Their zany but effective enforcement antics were enthusiastically covered by newspapers. The outgoing Izzy, in particular, was a media favorite. He was referred to as the "incomparable Izzy" and "America's premier hooch-hound." Izzy was proficient in a number of languages aside from English, including German, Yiddish, Polish and Hungarian. He was also able to get by in Italian, Russian and French. His ability to speak multiple languages proved to be an asset when working undercover. One of Izzy's

Izzy and Moe. *Library of Congress.*

favorite expressions when apprehending one of his suspects was "Dere's sad news here. You're under arrest." Another favorite was "Season's over" as he was arresting an unsuspecting bartender. The duo were masters of disguise, with a repertoire of over one hundred masquerades. In the course of their work, Izzy and Moe impersonated a plethora of personalities, including farmers, college students, gravediggers, streetcar conductors, firemen, truck drivers, football players and even man and wife. Izzy Einstein referred to his successful operations as the "Einstein Theory of Rum Snooping."

THE REPEAL OF PROHIBITION

I think this would be a good time for a beer.
—Franklin Roosevelt, March 12, 1933

At 3:32 p.m. on December 5, 1933, the Twenty-First Amendment, calling for the repeal of Prohibition, was ratified. The "noble experiment" known as Prohibition officially ended. Section 1 of the amendment simply reads:

Announcing the repeal of Prohibition. *Author's collection.*

A toast to the end of Prohibition. *Author's collection.*

"The eighteenth article of amendment to the Constitution of the United States is hereby repealed." December 5 became known as "Repeal Day."

So, what led to the demise of Prohibition in the United States? The answer lies in several key factors: a shift in public sentiment toward repeal, the effective push by women's groups and the Great Depression.

During the course of the Prohibition era, average citizens and many politicians began to see the unintended harm caused by Prohibition. Americans began to hear daily accounts of the widespread disrespect for the law (bootlegging, speakeasies and so on) and the corruption of many public officials. Tragic incidents like the shooting deaths of three crew members of the *Black Duck* rumrunning boat by the Coast Guard (even if justified) contributed to the shift in public sentiment toward repeal of the Prohibition Act.

The rise of organized crime was also a major factor in swaying public opinion toward repeal. On February 14, 1929, an outbreak of violence between rival bootleggers occurred in Chicago, Illinois. This extremely violent event was known as the Saint Valentine's Day Massacre. This one incident caused outrage throughout the United States. It was the main reason

Women's Organization for National Prohibition Reform at the Ballot Box. *Library of Congress.*

that motivated a Cleveland group known as "The Crusaders" to form as a Prohibition repeal organization. Other such groups began to form as the nation became weary of reading about the violence that was taking place and the criminal element getting more and more involved in the trafficking of illegal liquor.

What was once thought to be the nation's answer to the ills associated with alcohol was now viewed as an ineffective law. Despite the best efforts of law

Opposite: We Want Beer Parade. *Author's collection.*

Left: The Crusaders, an organization to repeal Prohibition. *Library of Congress.*

enforcement, many Americans had come to believe that the Prohibition Act had failed in keeping the pledge to adequately control the production, sale and transportation of illegal intoxicating liquors.

As a sign of the changing national sentiment in favor of Prohibition repeal, a crowd of an estimated 150,000 protesters organized for a "We Want Beer" parade on Saturday, May 14, 1932. The parade was inspired and led by New York City mayor Jimmy Walker. Led by Mayor Walker, the protesters marched down Fifth Avenue with signs that read "Beer for Taxation" and "We Want Beer." Business leaders, celebrities, military heroes and sports figures all took part in the march. The marchers chanted "Who Wants Beer—We Do!" Walker inspired similar parades held in other U.S. cities.

Interestingly, it was the push of women's organizations that was influential in the passage of the Eighteenth Amendment, and it was also influential women's groups that were pivotal in leading to the repeal of the Eighteenth Amendment. Most noteworthy was the Chicago-based Women's

Organization for the National Prohibition Reform (WONPR) organized on May 28, 1929. WONPR was founded by Pauline Morton Sabin, and its membership was well over one million. According to Sabin, "The prohibition law, written for weaklings and derelicts, has divided the nation, like Gaul, into three parts—wets, drys, and hypocrites."

Finally, and perhaps one of the most important reasons for Prohibition repeal, was the stock market crash and the oncoming Great Depression of 1929. With the country in such a dreadful economic situation, a logical place to get the revenue back was the tax on legal alcohol.

6

NELLIE GREEN

The Prohibition Years

Nellie Green had the touch of Midas and the temperament of Thor.
—Peter Cameron, friend of Nellie Green

Trusting her instincts, Nellie Green was convinced that her hotel and her other properties were strategically and ideally located for a lucrative bootlegging and rumrunning operation. As in the past, her instincts proved to be right on the mark. Nellie was very much aware that she was widely known, respected and trusted not only by the East Haven community but also throughout many areas of Connecticut and New York. Nellie had already been assured that she could count on the cooperation of many important and influential people, including bankers, merchants, politicians and even prominent members of local and state law enforcement.

When Nellie declared her intention to bootleg illegal liquor, her husband, Will, and her son, Charlie, were disturbed and concerned. They knew that Nellie had a plan. They also knew that once she made up her mind, nobody would be able to talk her out of it. Nellie did consult with both of them individually and jointly—and then she did as she pleased. It was always that way. Whenever Will tried to change Nellie's mind, to convince her to have nothing to do with the bootlegging business, her response was for Will to attend to his business at the Talmadge Boat Yard, the Talmadge Coal Company, his ice business and his garage—and she would attend to her bootlegging. She assured Will that she knew what she was doing. And before her son was able to protest any further, she ordered

Left: "Old Iron Horse" Nellie Green. Bedecked in her trademark long riding coat, derby hat and carrying a riding crop.

Below: Fleet of soda and near-beer vehicles in front of Ye Olde Bridge Beverage Company.

Charlie to attend to managing the soft drink business at the Ye Olde Bridge Beverage Company.

Nellie found a great deal of support within a number of Connecticut localities to start up her bootlegging business. The financial support came from numerous components and a diverse population:

> *When people heard that I was contemplatin' goin' into the bootleggin' business, the money started flowin' in from all over. It wasn't long before bankers, druggists, merchants and the like of that—big shots from New Haven—and lots of other such places began supportin' me in a financial way. They chipped in 20k, 10k, 5k, and even as low as 2,500k, the each of 'em, to start with. And they all said, "Give the cash to Nellie, let her handle it." We trusted one another, we had to. And it was like that all the way. Personally, I didn't put up nawthin, save, I guess it was later, I might buy five hundred cases over the rail for myself—to sell as I please, that is.*

At times, Nellie would make deals with certain law men so that both she and the law enforcers would get what they wanted. As an example, she talked about her dealings with a certain local judge. As Nellie put it, "So, he telephones me and he asks, 'Where is the special good beer comin' from?' I wouldn't tell him, so he got mad. He said, 'I got plenty on you, Nellie Green!' So, I said, 'And I got plenty on you, judge, if I started talkin'! I finally gave in and told him where the really good beer can be found. You can't argue with a judge, can you?" Later on, the judge would repay Nellie in another matter:

> *There was this mean state trooper who was always nosing around my place. He used to look around my boat, the Eda, when she came out to New Haven. He never found nawthin' but he became real intrusive. As a favor, the judge, had the trooper transferred to a different division. This is how it was done. This—at least—was one of the methods. And so in the end both the judge and me got what we wanted.*

On another occasion, Nellie worked closely with a U.S. marshal on a business transaction that benefited both of them:

> *There was this U.S. Marshall [sic]—I won't say the name – whose job it was to dispose of the trucks and automobiles which was knocked off*

by the federal people for rum running. They picked up a lot of these hi-falutin' trucks and cars and then put them up for auction on the grounds of the Smedley Company in New Haven. This company—they used to have storage rooms—and I hired the rooms. The company didn't never know what was in 'em. The cops and the Revenue men knew, but they were very kind. So this Marshall and I had an understandin' about these trucks and cars when they came up for auction. My son Charlie and I we'd go into the grounds where the auctions were held. My Charlie would go to the end of the line, and pretend like he was goin' to bid on these. Knowin' who Charlie was and what he represented, other possible bidders would follow him to try to outbid him. But, in actuality, Charlie was my decoy. The Marshall and I, having made a previous arrangement, would take advantage of the moment and I was able to get the trucks and cars I wanted. The Marshall and I then sold 'em for double, which was the plan, and split between us. It may have been wrong, 'specially as my Charlie was in on it, but that's the way it was. I won't never lie. And I want to tell it jest the way it happened.

So what was Nellie Green's role in her bootlegging operation? Nellie's main role as a bootlegger was to serve as a "drop" (a middleman). She put it this way: "I received loads of likker consigned to others, and got rid of them in a jiffy with minimum risk, which I liked." Her cut was five dollars per case of liquor, "for handlin'—that was the understandin'."

In situations that required her men to transport illegal alcohol across the state, she charged other bootleggers a fee of $2,500 per transport. Known mobsters (especially from New York) were aware of her ideal location off Long Island and near big cities like New Haven and Bridgeport. They approached Nellie on a number of occasions to join them on a permanent basis, but she turned down all those offers. She preferred her bootlegging business as is and had no interest in becoming involved with "those big shots in New York."

Nellie's bootlegging contracts were usually arranged on an off-the-cuff basis. The principles of trust, loyalty and honesty were important to her. She had a good sense of people who tried to con her and knew how to control these relationships while making a profit for herself.

Real names were replaced by nicknames, and all the while, Nellie trusted her gut instincts and savvy business knowhow. For Nellie, bootlegging was a risky, challenging and sometimes exciting adventure. She was very much aware of the rumrunning activities taking place in Rum Row and other places:

Them boats would be fully loaded with illegal cargo, carryin' one hundred thousand or more cases of Scotch, wines, beer, you name it. A few of the boats out there on the Row might be lucky and get rid of thousands of cases of alcohol in a couple of weeks or less, dependin' on prices and conditions ashore. Others would stay there for months. For the most part, I was able to dispose of a large amount of stuff fast, with the understandin' of my five dollars a case. If I couldn't get rid of the shipment fast I would bury the stuff til the coast was clear in Talmadge's coal bins where the big docks were a few hundred yards down the river toward Mansfield Point. This proved convenient on occasion. When my position was "hot" I would hide the booze on my premises in fake walls that nobody knew about, but that wasn't often 'cause the trucks were always waitin' to haul it all away. Before I knew it, I was makin' more money than I knew what to do with. It was then I realized that good ole Honorable Andrew J. Volstead was the goose that was layin' the golden eggs, and I had no intention of interfurin' with that!

Nellie felt justified in her defiance of the Eighteenth Amendment and in circumventing the "foolish" Prohibition law. She knew the difference between right and wrong when it pertained to bootlegging, but it was within her own code of ethics. Nellie believed that she was performing a valuable service to good people who were deprived of having a drink or two. At times, Nellie thought it was an exciting game to outwit law enforcement who tried to interfere with her business—and it was a lucrative business. Nellie liked to repeat a quote from a high-ranking judge who once commented to a member of his staff as they were having a drink, "You know, there's no such thing as a good law which good men disobey."

Nellie Green was known as the "Queen of Rum Row," a title she tended to downplay. Ironically, she despised rum, notwithstanding the fact that her grandfather, father, mother and she herself sold it. It was all part of the game.

Many readers may get a keen insight into the mindset of bootleggers and rumrunners by reading their personal encounters with Nellie Green and other people in the liquor trade at the time. In particular, Nellie discussed her adventures with three individuals she nicknamed "Cap'n Charlie," "Blackie" and "King Tut."

Cap'n Charlie

So jest to make sure, I grabbed the gun and the gat and throwd 'em, loaded and all, into the Farm River.

—Nellie Green

At one point, Nellie Green had business dealings with a man she referred to as "Cap'n Charlie." As you will see, Cap'n Charlie was a well known and controversial figure who was a prominent bootlegger turned Prohibition agent turned bootlegger. Actually, Nellie had a few other nicknames for this individual, including "Charlie the Con" and "Cap'n No Account."

Early on during the Prohibition period, well-known organizations began to contact Nellie Green about becoming partners in various bootlegging operations. As Nellie said, "The Big Shots from outside the state and all over began telephonin' me, with my not knowin' who they were or what they were after." One such "big shot" was Cap'n Charlie. Nellie recalled one encounter with Cap'n Charlie:

> *He seemed to be runnin' things in New York. He had suites at the Commodore, the Astor, and he moved about a good deal. And he propositioned me about what he could do. But I told him I didn't talk with no strangers on the telephone. When he asked me to come down to New York, I told him, and plenty plain, that if he wanted to talk with me, he could damn well trot up to Farm River, if his feet weren't hurtin', and explain exactly what he had on his mind. And, anyway, how did he get my name?*

Nellie continued,

> *He started to tell me all the stuff he had, and about the trucks runnin' from Pennsylvania, down Philadelphia way, and claiming he was a "partner" of the Govner. I told him, yes I remembered the Govner, I met him in Washington when I was twenty-three. So I told him to cut it short and come on up if he was a-comin' or hang up and shut up and stop the blah-blah-blah! So he said, all right, he'd come up, but he'd call my bluff, and I told him jest try it!*

And so Cap'n Charlie did show up in East Haven, ego deflated after being "dressed down" by Nellie Green. Nellie's first impression of Cap'n Charlie was not favorable, to say the least. It became immediately apparent to him that Nellie's "greeting" was not what he anticipated, certainly not what he was used to back in New York and other places he had done business. Nellie Green, as was her style, was not about to take any "guff" from him or anyone else for that matter. As Nellie explained, "So here comes Cap'n Charlie in his city slicker outfit. He talked big, he acted big, and at first sight, I didn't like him. He said, in a boastin' manner, he could deliver five thousand cases from Rum Row. I told him I'd settle for five hundred and then see what was what."

With a wary eye and an instinctive distaste, Nellie agreed to do business with Cap'n Charlie. But, as she explained,

He wasn't a partner, exactly, we just made deals having to do with this and that—for about two years. Deals for the delivery of no fewer than five hundred cases, often one thousand cases and more. And so, when I heard a boat comin' up the river, I had a feelin' it was the first load of five hundred cases, and I was gettin' five dollars a case for movin' it. So I run down to the dock where the boat was pullin' in and my husband Will yells at me "You fool you can get shot, you come back in the hotel." But I told Will to go back into the house and mind his own business. I knew what I was doin', so I went out to meet them.

The first man to get off the boat was Cap'n Charlie himself. When he went to shake my hand the first thing I noticed was that he had a gun slung over his trench coat, and a pistol that was almost as big as the gun, which was strapped on his hip. So I said to him, cuttin' all the formalities, "You take that gun off your shoulder, and that gat off your hip, before someone sticks one of 'em up your behind and pulls the trigger, which will be the end of you! Ain't nobody comin' around here with guns or gats or nawthin' like that. We run a place decent and respectable."

And so Cap'n Charlie, after shootin' off his mouth as to no account, he takes 'em off and he puts 'em up against a bin which wasn't satisfactory to me. So jest to make sure, I grabbed the gun and the gat and throwd 'em, loaded and all, into the Farm River. After that, he acted kind of normal considerin' what he was and where he came from, which I didn't know for sure but my gut feeling was tellin' me it was from a dark place.

As a guest in the Hotel Talmadge, Cap'n Charlie became very comfortable and began making friends with many other patrons of the hotel. As Nellie said, "He would brag about his private airplane, his fishing boats, speedboats, tugboats, and his big Packard, or maybe it was a Hudson, that was chauffeured." But there was one person who he feared and eventually learned he would neither be able to impress nor control—Nellie Green, who he always referred to as Mrs. Talmadge. Nellie told it like this:

> *One day, Cap'n Charlie comes down to the bar with two hookers he secretly hired and takes a wad of bills, scatterin' fifties, hundreds and five hundreds all over the place trying to impress. So I told him to pick up all your filthy, dirty money and put 'em where the monkey put the marbles. A feller with ten cents is as good as the likes of you aroun' here—any time and most of the time! Big Shot or no Big Shot, "Cap'n No Account" didn't make no impression on me, if that was what he was aimin' at. Cap'n Charlie said that he had travelled far and wide but that he had never met the likes of me. Ain't that the truth!*

Nellie referred to her mother as "well-schooled and a reader of all printed works." Unlike her mother, Nellie instead trusted and relied on her gut instincts. She did this all her life, whether in business dealings or in other life situations. What she lacked in formal education she more than made up for with her instincts about people, especially people who did not have her best interest in mind. She immediately formed a dislike and distrust in those individuals. And one of those individuals was Cap'n Charlie. He would often brag about controlling many boats out on Rum Row. Nellie wasn't impressed and really didn't care. She suspected that he did have a number of vessels out on the Row but never asked him.

As she asserted,

> *It must've been quite a few boats because he landed thousands and thousands of cases of stuff all along the shore between here (East Haven) and Boston, Providence, Fall River, and such. And some of it went over the road into the interior, and God only knows where it went after that. He had scouts through there I knew nawthin' about. I didn't have nawthin' to do with them people. What business he and I did was done right here on Farm River. He'd buy from Rum Row and sell to Rum Row, and he had boats out there himself, and people would go out there and get it from him over the rail. And so, the stuff would come in from Rum Row and bang out it went, right quickly I would add. I know that most of it was prime whiskey. I would pay thirty dollars (or thereabouts) per case, over the rail, and sold it to wholesalers as high as a hundred and twenty-five. I've heard that some people called me "the Queen of Rum Row" but I was not sure of that title because I was never out on Rum Row, not once.*

Connecticut Bootlegger Queen Nellie Green

Had Nellie been a "reader" like her mother, she would have discovered proof of why her gut instincts about the man she called "Charlie the Con" were correct. At the same time that Nellie was making "cautious" deals with this man who she neither trusted nor respected, the print media was telling a story of a man who, for a time, successfully worked both sides of the Prohibition law.

Using several aliases, Cap'n Charlie began his illegal liquor activities at the very beginning of Prohibition. He soon became a prominent bootlegger in a number of states, heading a million-dollar rum smuggling business. Among other things, federal law enforcement claimed he was the mastermind of a gigantic liquor smuggling ring, transporting illegal whiskey to the United States from the Bahamas and also from Scotland by way of Nova Scotia. When he was finally captured by Prohibition agents, he made a deal with the feds. The immunity deal, which law enforcement accepted, was that he would provide all names and information concerning his smuggling business in exchange for becoming a national law enforcement undercover agent himself. When he testified in court as an agent, the print media referred to him as the "Mysterious Charlie" since he was not recognizable to his "captors" because of his undercover disguises. But once again, Charlie conned the law enforcement bureau by continuing to smuggle liquor on the side (at the same time he was working with the Prohibition officers!). The con continued until it was brought to the attention of the Department Chief John D. Appleby, who eventually fired him from the Prohibition Bureau.

Nellie had plenty of opportunities to greatly expand her bootlegging business. Many large bootlegging organizations throughout the East Coast were itching to become partners with Nellie, realizing the unique location of her establishments on East Haven's Farm River. But Nellie was satisfied with her current bootlegging operation which was proving to be very productive. She did allow them to drop off their liquor for her to "move out quickly," providing they pay her the requisite five dollars per case. Thousands of cases of illegal alcohol were dropped off to Nellie as a result of this deal. This proved to be another lucrative transaction.

For a time, after no longer doing business with Cap'n Charlie, Nellie began making deals on her own. She hired men to transport many cases of liquor inland to other states using several large Buicks that she owned. Nellie's men had many encounters with Prohibition agents, including shootings at their cars. (Nellie did not allow her men to be armed.) But on many other occasions, she received "cooperation" from local law enforcement and local politicians, many of whom were frequent patrons of her hotel on Farm River.

BLACKIE

A lot of the rum money—hundreds of thousands—was kept secretly by an
ole lady—my cook. And nobody would ever dream of touchin' her!
—Nellie Green

Prior to forming her own fleet of rumrunning vessels with "Wing" St. Clair
as the captain of the crew, Nellie dealt separately with other rumrunners and
even formed a partnership with a few. One such rumrunner was a man known
only as "Blackie." Unlike with Cap'n Charlie, Nellie felt that she could trust
Blackie, whom she referred to as "fearless." He was not only fearless but also
an intelligent individual, which helped him get out of many difficult situations.

Blackie was a member of the famed Caterpillar Club, an elite club
consisting only of people who successfully used a parachute in a life-
threatening emergency to bail out of a disabled aircraft at the last minute.
The Caterpillar Club was formed in Ohio in November 1922, and among
its members are notables such as John Glenn, Jimmy Doolittle, George W.
Bush and Charles Lindbergh.

Having had experiences like this, Blackie showed no fear, and he considered
rumrunning a bit risky but also a fun and exciting "cat and mouse game."
As Nellie's rumrunner, Blackie would normally drop off her cargo of illegal
alcohol at the docks of the Talmadge Coal operation.

Like many of his rumrunner counterparts, Blackie considered members
of the Coast Guard as "enemies at sea—and good friends ashore." Bearing
no grudges, Blackie would have a drink or two with the same Guardsmen
who were assigned the task of chasing him and his rumrunning crew on
the waterways.

So here is Blackie recounting—in his own words—his adventures as a
rumrunner for Nellie (and others) and also his cat-and-mouse game with the
U.S. Coast Guard:

In the early days of Prohibition, the Coast Guard tried valiantly to capture
our speedboats but we were just too fast. Many times they would have to
give up. We had to run between a number of risky points in order to get
to Nellie Green's place on Farm River. Nellie was one of a kind. I really
respected her and enjoyed working with Nellie. If the Coast Guard really
chased us hard, we'd drop fishnets and foul up their propellers.

The Coast Guard would hear us coming, switch on their search lights,
and start giving it to us with their one-pounders, but that was like trying

to hit flying ducks with a small rifle. One night in a tavern ashore, a Guardsman says to me "one of these nights, I'll get you!" I simply responded "Chum, with those one-pounders of yours, you couldn't hit the other side of the street, zeroed in and broadside." The guardsmen and us guys would have a lot of laughs and fun onshore. On the waterways, it was different as they had their job to do and I understood that.

The Guardsmen never bothered us much in the early days. We just outran them. We'd outstrip them. My engineers—two fearless Georgia boys—used to hold their hands up in the searchlight when their shells came screeching over and the boys made as if they were trying to catch one of the shells and laugh. But I told them they wouldn't laugh if they ever did catch one of those shells. The risks were high and the money was good—but really, for us it was the thrill of the chase.

It wasn't too long before things got tougher for us. The Coast Guard and the Customs Service brought in large subchasers with powerful engines, and large destroyers with potent guns. The destroyers were bad news for us. And they didn't hesitate to use their guns, either. The destroyers were based in New London, Connecticut. They worked mostly offshore out around The Fleet. We respected 'em. I soon realized that if they hadn't been a bit on the friendly side, they could have put us out of business at any time, had they really set their minds on it. I've said it before, and I repeat it, we were enemies at sea—and damned good friends ashore. Many's the meal I had aboard a Coast Guarder, with the skipper and his crew—who were shooting at us the night before.

Sometimes they'd lay off in the haze, and then, when they heard us coming, they'd close in. We'd run like hell away from them. The seas would hide us and we'd wait, with our engines off, and lay low, and then, after they lost us, we'd go back and resume loading. We called such maneuvers "hit and run."

Hijackers on the open sea were always a concern for Blackie and other rumrunners, as he pointed out:

The G-men and the bootleggers hated hi-jackers. Hated them equally. One of the hi-jackers we encountered—call him Bud—was actually a decent fella. Christ, what guts that guy had! Once, Bud took over a liquor warehouse in Providence and, at the point of a gun, made the cops help him load his trucks and steer him where he wanted to go. Bud owned a big and fast yacht. He carried hand grenades, dynamite bombs, and high-powered *rifles. And he wouldn't hesitate to use them if he felt he had to. At heart he was a pirate, but sometimes pirates can be swell guys.*

In fact, Blackie and "Bud" were friends when not on the open seas and even had dinner on the hijacker's yacht on a number of occasions. As Blackie often said, "Enemies at times, friends at other times!"

Blackie talked about his encounter with a noted Coast Guard patrol boat:

The flagship of the Coast Guard at the time was the Red Wing, *a converted mine sweeper. She would throw powerful shells at us. One night, the* Red Wing *gave us a tight chase. My engineer—what nerve that guy had—helped me run her on the shoals, with her deeper draft, the same as we did with other Coast Guard vessels. It was a tricky maneuver but my engineer managed to do it. The* Red Wing *couldn't run the shoals. I'm tellin' ya, boy, those were neck-and-neck chases.*

It was the law that the Coast Guard could intercept any American registered vessel suspected of being a smuggler within *the imposed Rum Line limit—the boarder* [sic] *that separated U.S. territorial waters from international waters. Initially, the Rum Line was 3 miles from shore, then moved to 12 miles from shore. Anything further than the Rum Line was considered international waters and, therefore, the U.S. Coast Guard had no jurisdiction in the international waters. If intercepted by the Coast Guard or Customs people, we rum runners would simply destroy our receipts and papers we knew would be of value to the Coast Guard. If needed, we could always get duplicates of our receipts.*

When things began to get really tough, we set up a large yacht on the Rum Line, visible to the Coasties. The yacht never had any liquor aboard. While the Coast Guard sub-chasers were going over this yacht in great detail, we'd go through the stretch of water to our destination.

Late one evening, while my boat was taking a load of liquor and I was having tea and biscuits with the captain of a Canadian schooner, I heard one of the crew sing out "Cutter alongside!". It was the Coast Guard Cutter the Tampa. *Visibility was poor. It was hazy. It was as close as I could touch her, almost. My boat, the* Dick *(a powerboat which cost $75,000 for her hull alone), was lying on the starboard of the Canadian schooner—that is, the Canadian schooner was between the* Tampa *and my speed boat. I knew the* Tampa *would not fire across the Canadian schooner. When the light was right, we pulled out and ran for it. And the* Tampa *opened up with her three-inch shells. But they never hit us. We* *raced forty miles to Shagwong Reef (Suffolk County) before we got clear away from her, and my outstanding recollection of this incident is my mate's comment, "Ain't she the shootin' bastard!"*

Blackie credited a local policeman for providing him with very sound advice. Whether the advice was warranted or not is open to debate. "This particular cop advised me that when we were going over the road in our cars, with our loads, not to mind if the federal or state police shot at us, because they didn't really want to do it. But, you'd better look out for the city cops—they shoot to hit!"

In a lighthearted moment, Blackie talked about another rumrunner out of Long Island. "He owned a fifty-six-footer vessel, and he made quite a lot of money rum running. One night as he was taking a nap, he heard heavy footsteps approaching. He sang out 'Quiet men, don't make so much God-damn noise! The troopers may be around!' Through the distance came the two word response, 'They are.'"

As an experienced rumrunner, Blackie was familiar with life on Rum Row and encounters that some of his fellow rumrunners dealt with, sometimes fatal.

Everybody in the business knew about the Black Duck. *She was a rum runner but she was unarmed. One night a Coast Guard cutter machine-gunned her and killed three members of her crew. A few nights later, an unidentified boat slipped up alongside a certain Coast Guard cutter and let her have it, point blank, and killed one of her crew in his bunk. That started a feud, which in many people's mind, meant the end of rum running.*

Blackie continued, "Most of the liquor we got from Rum Row would be brought to New York, the thirstiest of seaport cities. And all of us rum runners were familiar with the successful adventures of Bill McCoy, the founder of Rum Row. The 'Real McCoy,' that's for sure!"

Blackie and his crew were never caught, and his boats were never captured, despite the hundreds of rumrunning outings they made. Reflecting on his relationship with other rumrunners, Blackie commented "All in all, I have to say, there was a lot of honor between the boys in this game. Their word was as good as gold. We trusted each other. We had to."

While rumrunning for Nellie Green, Blackie unloaded his cargo of liquor at the Talmadge Coal dock. Blackie enjoyed working for Nellie, whom he called "a tough but fair women who I respected. She certainly was one of a kind."

Nellie made a tremendous amount of money with Blackie as her rumrunner. She hid hundreds of thousands of dollars in a secret location. As Nellie admitted, "A lot of the rum money was kept secretly by an ole lady—my cook. And nobody would ever dream of touchin' her!"

Bootlegging was a profitable business, and bootleggers like Nellie Green were ingenious people. While a good deal of money was made by smuggling illegal alcohol, many bootleggers and rumrunners admitted that the excitement had more to do with the thrill of the chase or, as Blackie called it, "a fun cat and mouse game."

And so, for many rumrunners, the emphasis always seemed to be how they did it, how they got away with it, rather than the financial gain they got out of it.

King Tut

You see, him living in a minister's cottage where I could store the liquor until I can move it, was very convenient and safe both for King Tut and me. The Feds would not go near a minister's home.

—*Nellie Green*

On another occasion, Nellie was approached by a gentleman from Nassau, Bahamas, whom she described as "a common, ordinary lookin' man." He sought Nellie out to inquire if she would be interested in being the "drop" for five thousand cases of really good liquor he had on Rum Row. At first Nellie was skeptical, but she sent "one of the boys" out to the Row to check on the liquor that the man alleged to be there. Sure enough, the man came back and verified that the Bahamian did have five thousand cases of alcohol and it was all good liquor. So Nellie made a deal with this man, giving him the name "King Tut." The arrangement consisted of five thousand cases of liquor to be delivered by King Tut to Nellie, as his drop, every month. Nellie's cut was $5 per case for "handlin'." King Tut also agreed to pay Nellie an additional $5,000 per week for the rental of one of Nellie's speedboats.

Nellie confirmed that the "deal was five thousand cases at five dollars per case, for handlin' every thirty days. He also agreed to pay me five thousand a week for the rental of my speedboat the *Eda*." Also in the deal was that he would take orders from Nellie only by telephone. For further security, a secret code would be used when they talked on the phone.

Nellie was very protective of King Tut and, of course, her cases of illegal liquor.

> *I made up my mind to keepin' him strictly under cover and away from the mob. And so I fixed him and his wife up in a Minister's cottage in Short Beach Branford. King Tut became well acquainted with the people in Short Beach, like as if he was a church member. But no one ever really knew who or what he was, not even at my place, except "the boys." All transactions were made in secret. You see, him living in a minister's cottage where I could store the liquor until I can move it, was very convenient and safe both for King Tut and me. The Feds would not go near a minister's home.*

Once again, Nellie's off-the-cuff financial agreement proved to be a highly profitable transaction. As Nellie put it,

> *It was an affair of honor between us, he trusted me and I trusted him. The money was put in the New Haven Merchants Bank in my name. The money began to go up to much more than $100,000, and it was just layin' there in cash, all of it. I could have taken advantage of him, but I didn't. I often wonder what I might have done to him if there had been anythin' crooked in me. How I could have taken advantage of him and all that money. But I didn't, I couldn't. The government (the revenue men), they caught up with this—they search bank accounts, you know—and I had to pay the tax, since it was in my name, but that was alright.*
>
> *Anyway, he took his money back to Nassau. He was so thankful that I helped him move the loads and I was happy for him. And so he came back to East Haven, at least every month (he flew back and forth). He shipped up a load of 5,000 cases, at least once a month, which I handled.*

Nellie's "understanding" friends in the police force (federal, state and local) would occasionally get word to her that a raid was forthcoming. Upon receiving advance notice of an upcoming raid, Nellie would simply have her men transfer all the illegal booze to the large cellar of the minister's cottage where King Tut was staying. Once the police showed up at the Hotel Talmadge, they would find no trace of alcohol and would signal to their commander that the coast was clear. Nellie admitted, "Raids like that were a bit upsetting to the hotel operations but I understood. They had to do their job—and I did mine."

Left: King Tut and his wife.

Below: Nellie's Number 1 House (*middle*), sometimes used as a speakeasy.

The hotel was closed down for a brief time on one occasion as a result of a raid that uncovered a small bottle of liquor that was mistakenly left behind. Nellie recalled that "they put a 'plaster' on the back door, where the customers come in." But even that didn't stop Nellie from serving her customers. Once the authorities locked up the Hotel Talmadge, Nellie had the word spread that liquor was available at the bar of her other locations on her premises—namely the Driftwood, the Number 1 House (another speakeasy) and the Dyke House Inn.

At one point, King Tut had his boat overtaken by two former crewmen while they were in Nassau. Nellie explained,

King Tut had a run-in or sump'n with the engineer and fireman (crew member). As a result of this dispute he let them go. But somehow they managed to sneak onboard the boat, after the schooner had been loaded. They concealed themselves in the cargo space when the boat set out to sea with its precious load, eatin' nawthin' but grains and nippin' a little of this and a little of that to nerve themselves up to what they was a-plannin' to do.

When the boat was off Pebble Beach, Florida the two men came on deck and stuck up the captain and his engineer, and they chased the other crew members up the mast with their loaded pistols, and took over. In other words, puttin' it plainly, they high-jacked King Tut, and they run her in to where they could unload the stuff and land it. They was a-goin' to sell it quickly, and for all I know they had someone in cahoots with 'em ashore. However, one of the crew members managed to escape after he had rowed in with a load, and he run to the police and tole 'em what was happenin'. The police, they come out with an ocean-goin' tug, the Three Friends, *I think it was, and arrested the hi-jackers and pulled the boat in. The hi-jackers, they went to prison, but the police couldn't put "plaster" on the boat [they couldn't seize the boat], or seize the cargo, because, you see, she had papers clearin' her for a Canadian port, legitimate. That's the way it was. They had papers protectin' 'em, but instead of unloadin' in Canada they'd stop off in Rum Row. That's the way it always was.*

There was a hell of a lot of fuss over all of this. We, up here in East Haven, didn't know what to make of it, and least of all King Tut. His boat jest didn't come in. She was long overdue. So, King Tut had to fly back and look into it and go to Florida and through all the fuss and feathers which was in it for him, and get in on the trial of that engineer and that fireman which had hi-jacked the boat.

Well, all I know in particular is that when the trouble was finally fixed up, the schooner had to go back to Nassau and reload. But, in their hurry to get the stuff ashore, and with all the rumpus, more than $20,000 worth of stuff was wasted—lost overboard or broken, and we had to make it good, we had to chip in. Of course, in this business you kind of expected accidents like this to happen, you can't always win. It's like betting on a horse. Somethin' jest got to go wrong somewhere, as it does in everyday life. And so, after we found out all about it, and put things right, it didn't bother us so much. We jest had the boat re-loaded and brought her up the way she should have come in the first place. I never knew how many boats King Tut had in Rum Row, and I didn't care, just as long as he kept sending the schooners up from Nassau, and I can handle their loads averaging about 5,000 cases a month. The money was always a-flowin', which was fine with me.

Occasionally, an acquaintance who worked up the nerve would ask Nellie, "How did you get away with it?" Nellie's response would always be "I'd rather not talk about it." But occasionally she did confide in her closest friends—although in a vague manner—how she managed to get away with things like this. "A certain amount of money (lots of money) was paid to a couple of important people to have two cops put on the police force who would mind their own business. Never mind what police force it was, that doesn't matter. The money was passed in cash at this place or that. It took a good deal of doing." And so, even though it was costly, transactions like this worked very much in Nellie's favor. And everyone involved was happy and content.

Wing St. Clair

My boats were sure fast, outrunnin' every one of those boats the Coast Guard had—and, of course, I had Wing St. Clair

—*Nellie Green*

Nellie began purchasing her own boats to be used in rumrunning. She built up a fleet of nine vessels: the *Eda*, the *Uno*, the *Onward*, the *Rosebud I*, *Rosebud II*, *Rosebud III*, the *Betty T*, the *Primrose* and the *Sparkle*. Some of her vessels were built by her husband, William Talmadge, and his men at the Talmadge boatyard near the hotel. The sixty-foot boats were equipped with two high-power surplus Liberty aircraft engines. The boats were stored in a variety

Frank "Wing" St. Clair standing with Betty Talmadge.

of locations, including the docks adjacent to the hotel and the boatyard operated by William Talmadge. The speedy vessels ran low in the water and could easily outrun anything the Coast Guard sent after them, especially over the Rum Line limit that defined territorial waters back then, beyond which the Coast Guard had no jurisdiction.

The rumrunning fleet was led by "Wing" St. Clair, Nellie's trusted and fearless rumrunner. St. Clair earned his nickname when he lost his right arm struggling to beach his boat on Orient Point, Long Island, in order to avoid the Feds. Wing was a close friend of Nellie and the Talmadge family. He would always dress in black since his rumrunning usually occurred at night, and the dark clothes made it more difficult for the Coast Guard to spot him, especially in fog. As the captain of Nellie's fleet, St. Clair would prove to be a valuable asset in the rumrunning business.

The *Eda*, one of Nellie's rumrunner boats.

The *Onward*, rumrunner boat.

The *Uno*, rumrunner boat.

The *Betty T*, rumrunner boat.

Nellie's husband (William Talmadge) behind the wheel of one of Nellie's boats with his son Charlie looking on.

The *Primrose*, rumrunner boat.

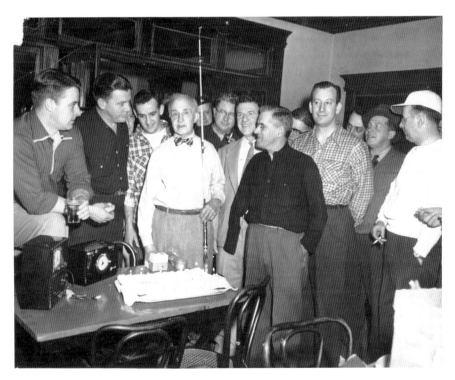

Nellie's lead rumrunner "Wing" St. Clair with cohorts.

Crew member Charles Hilton (*far left*), Nellie's son and her husband (*far right*) and an unidentified elderly person steering.

As per Nellie's instructions, St. Clair and his men were never permitted to be armed when they performed their rumrunning activities. Their mission was to work fast and efficient, load the boats quickly and then use both their speedboats and their gifted boating abilities to outrun law enforcement and the ever-present hijackers on the open seas. Wing and his crew made a lot of money for Nellie Green.

St. Clair never got caught, but one of his lieutenants did. One day, as Nellie was leaving for New Hampshire, she drew her crew's attention to the fact that several members of a new road repair crew were wearing shoes that were not suited for that kind of work. Once again, her uncanny instinct kicked in. Nellie passed this on to her crew: "Look at them shoes, they ain't no repairmen. They could be Feds." Worried that the men were undercover federal agents, Nellie instructed the crew that no landing was to be attempted until the all-clear signal was given by St. Clair. But after two days of idling offshore, the skipper of the *Sparkle* got restless and came in anyway. The Feds caught him red-handed at the dock. But with Nellie out of town, her husband, Will, was forced to take the rap.

The six-foot (and sometimes much higher) Farm River tides made routine navigation challenging but were at times an asset for a skillful rumrunner. It took a steady and knowledgeable hand to navigate the currents and eddies, especially at night, and Wing was just the man to negotiate the rough waters.

Despite Nellie's attempts to keep her activities as lowkey as possible, she became known as the "Queen of the Fastest Rumrunners on the East Coast." Nellie agreed, saying, "My boats were sure fast, outrunnin' every one of those boats the Coast Guard had—and, of course, I had 'Wing'. In my mind, there was no one more skilled and more trusted than Wing St. Clair."

Nellie had a fleet of nine rumunning vessels. Shown here are several boats owned and used by the crew of bootlegger Nellie Green.

7

THE SINKING OF THE *SPARKLE*

A "James Bond" Adventure

Son, do you know who I am?
—Nellie Green

S leep did not always come natural to Nellie Green. Such was the case when on a clear midnight she looked out the window of her second-floor suite in the Hotel Talmadge and caught sight of eight figures who had boarded her boat *Sparkle*. Looking closer, she saw what appeared to be state troopers. But why were they on the *Sparkle* at midnight? Instinctively, Nellie figured she was being framed. At this point, the *Sparkle* had been used to transport only near-beer, which was allowed under the Eighteenth Amendment.

So why were these troopers searching the *Sparkle*? Nellie instantly suspected an inside job. She and Will had been increasingly suspicious of her hotel manager at the time, "Mr. Jones" (name changed to protect his identity). It was this person who Nellie believed tipped off the state police and who was setting her up for trouble. But what could they possibly find except for the legal near-beer? The Coast Guard had targeted the *Sparkle* many times and inspected the boat for illegal liquor, but each time the Guardsmen discovered it contained only cases of legal near-beer and allowed the *Sparkle* to continue on its way. As Nellie explained,

No matter how often in all the time the Sparkle *ran across to Long Island with her load of 1,900 cases, more or less, covered with canvas on deck, right on deck clearly marked Olde Bridge Beverage Bottling Works, no matter how many times the Coast Guard flagged her down and inspected her, it was always the same—she carried nawthin' but near-beer, which was right and proper. They never got nawthin' on her and they never got nawthin' on my son Charlie. When the* Sparkle *nosed in to Talmadge's coal dock with about one hundred and twenty-five cases of rotten Scotch, the State Police from Westbrook was a-waitin' to receive her.*

Once again, Nellie's instincts proved to be correct. When Nellie went downstairs, she met up with one of the troopers "in the big room where the rock fireplace is, and where the public telephone is." Noticing that he was about to use the phone, Nellie asked the trooper,

"What's goin' on here?" So the trooper responds "It ain't nawthin' concernin' you, Mrs. Talmadge." So I tole him that anythin' and everythin' which happens aroun' my place concerns me and, God damn it, what is it? He said it was a boat called the Sparkle, *and she had come in with a load, and they had been tipped off, and they were summoned there to receive the boat for inspection. But first they needed a warrant which could take some time. He said for me to go back to bed and forget all about it. It didn't concern me in no way. But him bein' in and on my premises, at that hour, what with the boat bein' knocked off, did concern me. By this time I was wide awake and became aware that the boat captain was up in the hotel manager's bedroom a-gabbin' with him.*

Nellie continued, "So while the state copper was a-usin' my public telephone I went into my private office, where I had a private phone. I called my lawyer in New York and also a friend in Boston who had 'influence over these fellers.' My lawyer said he'd come up right away, it sounded like a frame-up to him."

While all this was going on, the state troopers began drinking the rotten scotch that was on the *Sparkle,* and they became intoxicated from all the drinking. "They were all drunk as skunks. They threw the empties in the river and, jest for the hell of it, shot at 'em with their pistols. The whole neighborhood heard 'em and they knew about it. They knew sump'n was a-goin' on, that is."

At this point, Nellie sprang into action. She assigned one of her men as a lookout at her Driftwood House, high up on the hill. She told the man to use his spyglass, "those big long telescopes we use to spy on boats at sea and see who they was." She posted another man in the cellar of the hotel, "so we could see every move they made while they was a-foolin' aroun' out there with the Sparkle, and still drinkin' the rotten Scotch, the stuff I'd been framed with."

Truth be told, Nellie was much more concerned that these troopers would begin nosing around and discover the $5,000 worth of liquor ("the best whiskey available") she had hidden all over the premises, including cases that were hidden in a big manure pile behind the old gray barn.

The troopers needed to leave—immediately. Nellie took immediate action and proceeded in a manner that James Bond would be proud of:

> And so, I swam out to the Sparkle as it was high tide and met the only crew member who didn't jump ship. He was a sixteen-year-old kid who looked miserable. I said to him "Son, do you know who I am?" He said "Yes, Ma'm, I know you." Now look, I said to the kid, I want you to do sump'n for me son. Don't you worry about nawthin'. I'll make sure you will be ok. "What do you want me to do, Mrs Talmadge?" Can you put the engine out of business, I mean, can you take some part of it so it won't run? "Yes Ma'm I could." And I asked the kid if he knew where the petcocks (shut off valve controls) are on the boat? "Yes Ma'm, I do." Would you be so kind as to take sump'n out of the engine, some vital part, so it won't run, and open the petcocks? Then jest you lay down and pretend you're drunk, like all the rest are, while she settles. I want the boat to go clear down to the bottom, see? Well, the kid done as I tole him. So the troopers start wakin' each other up not knowin' what was goin' on. And then the fun started! As I watched from my hotel window, they tried to get that engine to turn over—with its missin' part! Pretty soon, watchin' from my window, ol Sparkle slowly began to sink. The troopers jumped onto the deck, but some of them slipped and got all wet. I could see 'em stompin' their feet, shakin' their uniforms, a lookin' back at the Sparkle, amazed-like, a-wondering what in hell had happened to her. And I saw the young man with a big ol' knowin' smile on his face. Then—oh boy!—down she goes a-gurglin'! All I cared was to get the Sparkle to the bottom so the troopers couldn't take her out. That was my plan. You see, once she touched bottom, the state police had lost their jurisdiction, and she was then federal property. That was what I was aimin' for. That was what I was up to all the time when I was tryin' to figure out a way to get rid of the state troopers.

By having the *Sparkle* sink to the bottom of the river, Nellie knew the state police would have to give up their authority. As she said,

Once I knew the state troopers had left the premises, knowin' they no longer had jurisdiction, I telephoned the Custom House in New Haven and informed the authorities that a boat was on the bottom at Talmadge's coal dock. They asked what happened and I said I didn't know for sure, maybe she'd sprung a leak. The customs man asked what did I want them to do about it, and I said I want you to come down here at low tide and take the likker off, it ain't my likker. I ain't got nawthin' to do with that likker. That boat only carried near-beer, but no likker. The Custom House people did come down with a truck and picked up all the likker, appraising it at $5,000. I had the kid restore all the vital parts of the engine and close all the petcocks. After washin' the saltwater out and greasin', he started Sparkle *up again. The* Sparkle *was as good as ever!*

Nellie's plan worked like a charm. But with all the attention on the *Sparkle*, something else that needed her immediate attention arose:

My husband Will comes to me—he was tense—and says sarcastic like "You did a fine thing!" I asked, sarcastic like, what was it that was so fine? Talmadge said "Christ A'Mighty, don't you know all that stuff you got in the manure pile will heat up and blow up? Look at the sun spourin' down on it, and the steam!" Talmadge was right. Pretty soon—oh my God—it began to blow. Wham bang! It was explodin' all over the place, and showerin' the manure. You could smell it everywhere—the likker I mean. So that was sump'n else. So I had it all moved out, all that was left—in the broad daylight

For the most part, Nellie was fairly secretive as to where she stored her illegal liquor. As we have seen, she did admit to hiding her stuff in a secure place in the hotel, in fake walls in the hotel basement, in a minister's cottage and in a large manure pile (which didn't work out very well). But there were other places that Nellie stored her illegal booze, such as a nearby fireworks company that was safely secured behind barbed wire. It was a place people were reluctant to enter because of all the explosives.

Suffice it to say, it took a lot of ingenuity and guts on Nellie's part to safely secure the tremendous amount of liquor that was continually coming in and also to "negotiate" with law enforcement and others so that she could carry on her lucrative and well-loved Hotel Talmadge.

But many people learned long ago never to underestimate this amazing woman, who became known to many as a living legend.

8

PROHIBITION IN CONNECTICUT

*The assembly was unwilling to cede to the national government rights originally
reserved to the state under the constitution.*
—*Wilbur Cross, former Connecticut governor*

Connecticut was only one of two states not to ratify the Prohibition
Amendment. The Connecticut state senate had defeated ratification of
the Eighteenth Amendment by a vote of 20–14. The vote against ratification
was praised by a number of Connecticut newspapers, including the *Hartford
Courant* and the *New Haven Journal Courier*.

Throughout the Prohibition era, there were a number of groups
and individuals from Connecticut who were actively involved in the
nation's temperance, Prohibition and repeal movements. There were
also individuals associated with Connecticut who flaunted the Volstead
Act—engaging in bootlegging, rumrunning and frequenting speakeasies.
Here are a few examples.

P.T. BARNUM

*Alcohol is the greatest curse of the age; and there are few of my readers
who have not seen examples of the moral, mental, and physical ruin it
has wrought.*

—*P.T. Barnum*

When you hear the name P.T. Barnum, the first thing that may come to mind is "a great showman." And that he was, a theatrical promoter, an inspirational lecturer and founder of the Barnum & Bailey Circus.

Born in Bethel, Connecticut, Phineas Taylor Barnum was also a popular mayor of Bridgeport, Connecticut, and became the first president of Bridgeport Hospital, which he co-founded along with several others.

Perhaps a bit lesser known fact about Barnum is that he was a staunch supporter of the temperance movement in the Greater Bridgeport area. It did take a while for Barnum to become a temperance advocate—by his own admission, he was a drinker up until age forty. P.T. Barnum also served as chairman of the Committee of Temperance in Bridgeport.

THE GRISWOLD INN

The Griswold Inn (Essex, Connecticut) was very much a part of both the temperance and anti-Prohibition movements. As noted on the inn's website:

> *The Griswold Inn was the site of protests during the 1840's organized by the women of the "Temperance Movement." Several temperance banners remain from those protests, now hanging in the historic dining section of the Inn. For a time, The Griswold Inn itself became a "first class temperance hotel," although that doesn't seem to have lasted for very long. Even as the nation was turning toward prohibition in the early 20th century, the "Gris" was known as a reliable source for spirits. Often raided, occasionally fined and always back in business, the Federal authorities seemed to have had their hands full trying to stop the flow of liquor up the Connecticut River by "rum runners" at all hours of the night. These fast boats would dock on one of the many secluded coves along the river, unload, and be gone before anyone could track them down. The "Feds" were no match for the independent Yankee seaman who grew up on these waters.*

ELSIE HILL

Elsie Hill was a native of Norwalk, and she lived in several locations in Connecticut, including West Avenue and Woodlawn Avenue in Norwalk.

TEMPERANCE CONVENTION.

WITH Banner and with Badge we come,
An Army true and strong,
To Fight against the hosts of Rum,
And this shall be our Song.

THE STEAMBOAT

GREENFIELD

CAPT. D. W. REED, will leave HARTFORD, from the foot of Talcott-st., to-morrow morning,

WEDNESDAY,

October 27th, at 7 1-2 o'clock, for the purpose of conveying Delegates to the MASS CONVENTION, to assemble at MIDDLETOWN, at 10 o'clock of the same day—returning in the afternoon.

Fare each way, 25 Cents. — *Children half price.*

Mess. HAWKINS, POLLARD, WRIGHT, DWIGHT and other great apostles of Temperance are expected to be present and address the meeting. It is earnestly hoped that the *Washington* and *Young Men's* Temperance Societies of Hartford will be represented by a host of willing hearts and ready hands, upon this occasion.

Strike! 'till the last armed foe expires!
Strike! for the green graves of your sires,
God, and your native land!

Prohibition poster in the Griswold Inn. *Author's collection.*

Elsie attended school in the Norwalk area, was educated at Vassar College and was married to Albert Levitt (of Redding, Connecticut), who attended Yale University in New Haven.

Elsie played an active role at the Prohibition Party Convention in St. Paul, Minnesota, as a member of the Congressional Union for Woman Suffrage/Woman's Party. The Prohibition Party Convention took place on July 19–20, 1916.

Aside from suffragist issues, Elsie Hill played an active role in local issues, including the fight to expand Sherwood Island in Westport, Connecticut.

WILBUR CROSS

In his inaugural address to the Connecticut general assembly on January 8, 1931, Connecticut governor Wilbur Lucius Cross called for the repeal of the Prohibition Act. In his address, Cross stated the reason why Connecticut never ratified the amendment was because "the assembly was unwilling to cede to the national government rights originally reserved to the state under the constitution."

Cross was born in Mansfield, Connecticut, and he attended elementary school in Willimantic, Connecticut, was a principal at Staples High School (Westport) and attended and taught at Yale University. Wilbur Cross was elected as governor of Connecticut in 1930.

WILLIAM TAFT

I am opposed to national prohibition because I think it is a mixing of the national Government in a matter which should be one of local settlement.
—*William Taft*

William Howard Taft served as the twenty-seventh president of the United States, a Yale University professor (1913–21) and chief justice of the Supreme Court (1921–30).

While at Yale University, Taft opposed Prohibition before it passed in 1919, believing Prohibition should be left up to individual states and would be difficult to enforce on a national basis. As chief justice, however, Taft favored strict enforcement of anti-liquor laws as established in the Prohibition Act.

YE CASTLE INN

Ye Castle Inn of Old Saybrook, Connecticut, was widely known to serve illegal liquor to its guests during Prohibition. The inn was owned by Otto and Margaret Lindbergh (relatives of aviator Charles Lindbergh), who purchased the massive stone mansion in 1923. The Lindberghs converted the former private residence into an upscale hotel and restaurant.

With ties to influential politicians and New York–based organizations, the couple's son-in-law spearheaded one of the largest smuggling operations along the Connecticut coast. The alcohol cargo would come in on speedboats from the famed Rum Row and was distributed to drop-off points along the Connecticut River and Connecticut shoreline. With a fleet of five speedy rumrunning vessels and with the family's ties to powerful and influential people, the illegal smuggling continued for several years.

HOTEL TALMADGE

As we have seen, Nellie Green (Talmadge) ran a very profitable bootlegging operation out of her East Haven, Connecticut establishments. It was an ideal location for rumrunning. Nellie owned a fleet of nine speedy rumrunner boats led by Wing St. Clair, a trusted and fearless rumrunner. Nellie was known by many as the Queen of the Fastest Rumrunners on the East Coast.

BRIDGEPORT

Bridgeport, Connecticut, was a booming location during the Roaring Twenties. Many of the city's establishments flourished during this period. Actors, singers and flappers (for example, Mae West) appeared at such Bridgeport landmarks as the Ritz Ballroom, the Poli Palace and the Majestic Theater.

Bridgeport was also a hotbed of illegal liquor smuggling in the early 1920s. In October 1922, a huge illegal alcohol ring was uncovered in the Park City. Ironically, the person credited for busting up the illegal operation in Bridgeport was none other than the notorious bootlegger turned undercover Prohibition agent Nellie Green referred to as "Cap'n Charlie." This is the same person who was making bootlegging deals with Nellie Green while at the same time working as a Prohibition agent. Ironic, too, was the fact that he received praise from the Washington, D.C. Prohibition Bureau for busting up Bridgeport's illegal liquor ring. The bureau paid tribute to him, saying he used his former bootlegging experiences to capture the bad guys, not knowing that he was still bootlegging on the side.

LOIS LONG

No one represented the excesses of the Roaring Twenties decade better than Stamford, Connecticut native Lois Long. Educated at Stamford High School and Vassar College, Long wrote about the party scene in many New York City speakeasies under the pseudonym "Lipstick." She was an extremely popular reporter and critic for the internationally renowned magazine *The New Yorker*. Lipstick summed up her approach to life in the Roaring Twenties this way: "Tomorrow we may die, so let's get drunk and make love." Illegal alcohol was easily obtained during Prohibition and fueled the underground party atmosphere in New York City during the Roaring Twenties.

Lois Long (second row, far left) while at Vassar, editor of The Vassarion. *Author's collection.*

Lois Long married the famed *New Yorker* cartoonist and partygoer Peter Arno. Arno had a strong connection to Connecticut as well. He attended Hotchkiss School in Lakeville, Connecticut, and Yale University in New Haven.

BILL McCOY

According to media reports, famed rumrunner Bill McCoy, on several occasions, sailed his ship into Long Island Sound and ventured into Connecticut shoreline towns, where he unloaded his cargo at a pier there.

After his schooner the *Henry L. Marshall* was seized by the Coast Guard on August 2, 1921, McCoy was indicted because he was the owner of the vessel. McCoy secretly spent some time in New London, Connecticut, to check on five hundred cases of liquor that were removed by his men from

Bill McCoy. *Courtesy of the U.S. Coast Guard.*

his other vessel, the *Arethusa*. McCoy registered under an assumed name in a New London hotel. While he was in New London, McCoy sold his liquor to residents there as well as to customers in other parts of Connecticut. But once he got word that he was being tailed by law enforcement, McCoy, now a wanted man, fled to live in the Bahamas.

Ellery Thompson

Allegedly, Connecticut resident Ellery Thompson was of assistance to Bill McCoy on at least one occasion by sailing the famed rumrunner out from New London to his schooner waiting at Rum Row, just outside the Rum Line. McCoy's schooner had thousands of burlap sacks loaded with liquor, and he was in a rush to meet up with his boat.

Ellery Thompson was a fisherman, artist and writer. He lived in several Connecticut towns, including Mystic, Stonington, Groton and New London.

Fairfield County

During Prohibition, the coastline of Fairfield County (which included towns such as Westport, Bridgeport, Greenwich, Norwalk and Stratford) provided direct access to international waters. After picking up their cargo from places like Rum Row, the rumrunners would deliver their cases of illegal liquor to a number of locations on the mainland and various Fairfield County towns. Once the cargo was inland, the illegal alcohol was distributed to waiting establishments, usually along the long stretch known as the Post Road.

Warner Brothers Company (Bridgeport, Connecticut)

At one time, the Warner Brothers Company of Bridgeport, Connecticut, was a successful corset making firm. However, the flapper movement of the 1920s favored less restrictive fashions. Many women of the Roaring Twenties era had a more carefree attitude toward life and ditched the corset. This was a difficult time for the company, as it was not able to adequately adapt to these changing times. Sales declined dramatically.

DUTCH SCHULTZ

Notorious gangster Dutch Schultz once lived in Bridgeport, Connecticut. For a time, Schultz took up residence at the Savoy Hotel in Bridgeport and was often seen riding his horse Suntan in and around Fairfield (Bridgeport's neighboring town).

During Prohibition, Dutch Schultz purportedly was one of the biggest customers of Fairfield's infamous illegal liquor con man Philip Musica (a.k.a. Dr. F. Donald Coster).

FAIRFIELD

In the 1920s, Fairfield did not have a formal police department, only constables who had limited authority and found it very challenging to enforce the Prohibition law. Knowing this, illegal liquor violators felt emboldened to transport liquor through the town with very little interference. Fairfield finally organized its own police force in 1930.

The Fairfield Museum and History Center has on display a variety of liquor bottles from the Prohibition era. Pictured in the photo of the bottles of liquor are, from left to right:

◊ The first bottle (1920–25) was from Switzer Pharmacy of Southport (a former borough of Fairfield, Connecticut). The bottle contained "medicinal alcohol" and was not intended for non-medicinal consumption.

◊ Perry's Cider Brandy bottle. In 1920, local banker Francis Burr Perry was arrested and charged with manufacturing alcohol, along with other Prohibition-related infractions. A government raid on his property found seventy-seven thousand gallons of cider and wine. The charge of manufacturing alcohol was dropped, since Perry had a government permit.

◊ Glass liquor bottle. After Prohibition was repealed in 1933, Federal laws prohibited the reuse or sale of used liquor bottles. All liquor sold at that time was required to be in bottles that had the statement "FEDERAL LAW FORBIDS One Quart" embossed in the glass. This requirement was intended to discourage the reuse of bottles by bootleggers and moonshiners.

Bottles from Prohibition era. *Courtesy of the Fairfield Museum and History Center.*

JOHN HELD

Westport resident John Held became famous for his exaggerated illustrated drawings of flappers during the Prohibition era. The drawings came to symbolize the Jazz Age and appeared in popular magazines, including *The New Yorker*, *Vanity Fair*, *Harper's Bazaar* and *Life*. Held was a neighbor of F. Scott and Zelda Fitzgerald, and like the Fitzgeralds, he was well known for his lavish liquor parties at his beach cottage in Westport.

WESTPORT

Westport, Connecticut (like Fairfield), did not have an organized police department at the beginning of the Prohibition era (1920). For the most part, Westport's town officials did not cooperate with federal authorities in banning liquor. Westport became known for its lavish, heavy-drinking parties, especially during the early 1920s, and it was a haven for artists, writers and celebrities who openly defied the Volstead Act.

NEW HAVEN

Nellie Green and other bootleggers did a brisk business in the city of New Haven and the surrounding area. One New Haven bootlegger (identity withheld) was considered a chief source of the alcohol supply in Connecticut by law enforcement. He was sentenced to three to four years in state prison (Wethersfield, Connecticut).

BALD JACK ROSE

Notorious bootlegger and gambler Bald Jack Rose (born Jacob Rosenzweig) controlled rumrunning operations in Westport, Connecticut, in 1920. He was a Connecticut resident for a good part of his life, having lived in Bridgeport, Waterbury, South Norwalk and Westport. He also owned a gambling establishment in Norwich and was the founder of a minor league baseball team called the Rosebuds, which played in the now-defunct Connecticut League.

ORANGE

In 1925, five residents of Orange, Connecticut, were arrested on bootlegging charges after Prohibition agents uncovered a two-thousand-gallon still in a garage and seized thirty-nine five-gallon cans of alcohol.

CLINTONVILLE

In November 1925, Prohibition agents raided a Clintonville establishment and found twenty drums of illegal alcohol, each containing fifty gallons.

PHILIP MUSICA
(ALIAS DR. FRANK DONALD COSTER)

One of the most infamous illegal liquor con men of the Prohibition era was Philip Musica of Fairfield, Connecticut.

At the beginning of Prohibition, Musica was personally involved in several scam ventures that profited bootleggers and made him a very wealthy man. To add to his illegal activities, Musica used the alias Dr. Frank Donald Coster. He proudly boasted that he had obtained a doctorate and a medical degree from the University of Heidelberg (phony degrees that were part of the hoax).

In 1920, Musica founded the Adelphi Pharmaceutical Manufacturing Company in Brooklyn, New York. While Musica claimed that the main purpose of the company was to manufacture hair tonic and cosmetics, in reality it served as a major front for his bootlegging undertaking. In the 1920s, hair tonic and cosmetics used large quantities of alcohol. Although the law strictly controlled access to alcohol, Dr. Costa (Musica) managed to acquire a permit to obtain five thousand gallons of raw alcohol per month. He would then make a huge profit by selling large quantities of his tonic to bootleggers, who, in turn, distilled out the alcohol to make liquor and beer.

Musica later abandoned Adelphi, and in 1923, he began another company called Girard & Company. He moved his company from New York to his hometown of Fairfield. Still using his alias Dr. Frank Donald Coster,

Musica's new company produced products such as hair tonics, colognes and furniture polish that had a high alcohol content. With this company, he was allowed to obtain 5,200 gallons of alcohol per month. Some of his products had an alcohol content of 90 percent, which made them highly desirable to bootleggers. As was the case with his previous company, Musica sold his products to bootleggers who distilled out the alcohol to make illegal liquor. Musica also conned the Volstead Act enforcers to increase the number of gallons he was allowed to obtain. He did this by inviting the law enforcers to audit his company's books. The enforcers allegedly did a thorough audit, despite the fact that the books were mainly fraudulent. After the audit found no problems with the company, Dr. Coster's monthly alcohol allowance was increased from 5,200 to 25,000 gallons.

From his Mill Plain Road estate in Fairfield, Musica established close connections with racketeers and bootleggers throughout New England. Purportedly, gangster Dutch Schultz was one of his biggest customers. For a time, Schultz took up residence at the Savoy Hotel in Bridgeport (the neighboring city of Musica's hometown of Fairfield). Musica also paid for police protection to ensure the safety of trucks carrying alcohol away from his warehouse to their new destinations. Now a wealthy man living in a luxurious estate in Fairfield, Musica purchased a beautiful yacht, racing horses and a wide variety of luxury cars.

In 1926, he acquired McKesson & Robbins, which was a well-respected drug company. Musica's downfall would occur years later when massive fraudulent activities, which he masterminded, were uncovered at McKesson & Robbins. This was considered one of the largest corporate scandals of the early twentieth century. With law enforcement surrounding his home in Fairfield, Philip Musica took his own life on December 15, 1938.

Connecticut's Role in the Repeal of Prohibition

On November 8, 1932, Connecticut voters overwhelmingly approved the measure to repeal the Eighteenth Amendment. The measure that Connecticut residents voted on was shown on the state ballot as Question 3. The wording of the Question 3 petition read, "Calls for repeal of the 18th Amendment to the U.S. Constitution." The final statewide votes for repeal were "Yes," 292,787 (85.93 percent) and "No," 47,951 (14.07 percent).

Not surprisingly, the highest percentage of repeal votes came from Nellie Green's New Haven County (86.0 percent). The second-highest percentage was from Fairfield County, home of Westport and Bridgeport, towns known for high alcohol consumption. Voting percentages in the other Connecticut counties were Hartford County (83.6 percent), Middlesex County (81.1 percent) New London County (80.7 percent), Windham County (77.2 percent), Litchfield County (74.7 percent) and Tolland County (73.7 percent).

Prohibition received a chilly reception in Connecticut from the beginning to the end. It is clear that the prohibition of alcoholic beverages in Connecticut did little to stop its consumption in the Nutmeg State. Enforcement of the Volstead Act by the relatively low number of federal Prohibition agents assigned to the state was ineffective. Individuals and groups associated with Connecticut advocated fiercely for the repeal of the Prohibition Act. For example, two wealthy society women of Fairfield helped the cause of national Prohibition repeal by using their political ties and influence. One of these women was Annie Burr Jennings (born September 20, 1865), who inherited wealth through family investments. She was often referred to as the "First Lady of Fairfield." Jennings died on July 7, 1939, and was buried in Oak Lawn Cemetery in Fairfield, Connecticut. The other woman was Sylvia O'Dwyer, a graduate of Fairfield's Roger Ludlowe High School and Boston's prestigious Emerson College. Like Annie Jennings, O'Dwyer became very active in the Women's Organization of National Prohibition Reform, with a membership of over one million women.

Also, on June 15, 1919, Connecticut labor unions and city delegations joined a mass protest at the U.S. Capitol in Washington, D.C., to oppose Prohibition's Eighteenth Amendment. Connecticut was represented by city delegations from New Haven, Hartford, Waterbury and Bridgeport.

Despite the fact that Prohibition was repealed in 1933, three Connecticut towns—Wilton, Eastford and Bridgewater—stood firm and continued the ban on alcohol sales in their communities well beyond the year of repeal. In fact, it wasn't until 2014 that the remaining dry town voted to allow the sale of alcohol.

Wilton was the first of these three towns to allow alcohol sales. In 1992, Wilton restaurants were permitted to sell alcohol, and alcohol sales were allowed in package stores in 2010. Eastford was next with a vote to allow liquor sales in 2005. This left Bridgewater as the only dry town in Connecticut. Finally, on November 4, 2014, Bridgewater voted to allow the sale of alcohol in town limits.

Even after Prohibition was over, Connecticut law made it illegal to serve a woman alcohol at or within three feet of a bar for a long period of time. In 1969, the law was changed, and an act made it legal for women to "sit or stand" at bars.

9

THE REAL McCOY AND
THE PROHIBITION PIRATES

I have no tale of woe to tell you. I was outside the three-mile limit, selling whiskey, and good whiskey, to anyone and everyone who wanted to buy. I'm an honest lawbreaker.
—Bill McCoy, famed rumrunner

They were referred to as the "Prohibition Pirates" or, as they preferred to be called, "the aristocrats of the liquor trade." Many of them became legends—celebrities in their own right. Many Americans came to view them as the "swashbucklers of the twentieth century." I am referring to the elite group of expert seafaring navigators known as "rumrunners." And by far the most famous rumrunner in Prohibition history was Bill McCoy.

His father called him William
His mother called him Will
His sister called him Willie
But his crew called him Rummy Bill

—old jingle from McCoy's crew

William Frederick "Bill" McCoy was born on August 17, 1877, in Syracuse, New York. McCoy attended the Pennsylvania Nautical School on board the USS *Saratoga* in Philadelphia, graduating in 1895, first in his class.

At the very beginning of Prohibition in 1920, Bill McCoy (along with his brother Ben) was a boatbuilder in Jacksonville, Florida, earning a reputation

Famed rumrunner Bill McCoy wanted poster, June 16, 1921. *Author's collection.*

as a skilled yacht builder. His famous clients included the Vanderbilt family and Andrew Carnegie.

After hearing from an acquaintance about the possibility of a lucrative business in rumrunning, McCoy sold his business assets, traveled to Gloucester, Massachusetts, and purchased a fishing schooner called the *Henry L. Marshall* for $16,000. In McCoy's mind, the *Marshall* wasn't his ideal vessel for the rumrunning career he envisioned, but at least he was in the game.

McCoy's first liquor shipment was from the Bahamas to Savannah, Georgia, in 1921 and earned him $15,000. Realizing the potential for growth, Bill then set his sights on a 130-foot boat called the *Arethusa*, a thoroughbred vessel he called "the love of my life." He purchased the *Arethusa* for $21,000 (half its value) at auction. McCoy promptly replaced the engine with a much better smaller one, enabling his new vessel to travel at a much higher speed. He also increased the cargo space on the *Arethusa* to hold an additional one thousand cases, meaning that the *Arethusa* could now carry five thousand cases of liquor. The cargo was valued at $50,000—per trip. He also installed a machine gun on the deck of the *Arethusa*—to be used to discourage would-be hijackers.

To avoid U.S. jurisdiction, McCoy placed the *Arethusa* under British registry. Legally, the U.S. Coast Guard could not board a foreign ship if the boat was outside the three-mile limit of U.S. territorial waters. Bill renamed his prize vessel the *Tomoka* (the river that runs through Holly Hill, Florida, where he grew up). To further hide its identity, he registered the same boat with the French as the *Marie Celeste*. If the authorities got too close and wanted to take a photo of his vessel, he would quickly remove the *Tomoka* nameplate and screw on the name *Marie Celeste*. As noted by Assistant U.S. Attorney General Mabel Walker Willebrandt, "It is more difficult to handle rum running ships under foreign registry than under American."

McCoy then began to smuggle whiskey into the United States, traveling from Bimini and Nassau in the Bahamas to the East Coast of the United States. (For a time, he also smuggled liquor from the French islands of Saint-Pierre and Miquelon located south of Newfoundland.) As early as the spring of 1921, McCoy drew the attention of national law enforcement for his rumrunning activities.

Assistant U.S. Attorney General Mabel Walker Willebrandt. *Library of Congress.*

Whiskey cases awaiting rumrunners, Bimini Beach, Bahamas, 1921. *Library of Congress.*

Along with the *Tomoka* and the *Henry L Marshall*, McCoy added several other large rumrunning vessels to his fleet. His business on the waterways flourished, and McCoy soon became a household name, with his vessels carrying a wide assortment of the best liquors and wines. What set Bill McCoy apart from other rumrunners and what made him become famous was that McCoy sold only high-quality whiskey and scotch that was never "cut" (diluted). This was a much-prized commodity, since it was a common practice at the time to dilute liquor to increase the number of bottles for sale. McCoy also earned a reputation for fair dealing. Thus, his undiluted liquor and McCoy himself became known to his customers (and fellow rumrunners) as the "Real McCoy."

At the time of McCoy's rumrunning, there existed a three-mile U.S. maritime border. Vessels carrying loads of liquor beyond this three-mile limit were considered to be in international waters. Thus, the U.S. Coast Guard did not have jurisdiction to search and seize boats once inside the international waterways. This three-mile limit became known as the Rum Line.

McCoy came up with the brilliant idea to station his fleet of large vessels right at the edge of the three-mile limit of U.S. jurisdiction (but well within international waters) and sell his liquor there to smaller "contact boats" arriving from the mainland. The rows of anchored boats off the U.S. East

Coast became known as Rum Row. Bill McCoy is recognized as the founder of Rum Row, with the *Henry L. Marshall* being the first of the large vessels on the Row. Many large rumrunners followed suit, seeing the potential for huge profits. Think of these large Rum Row vessels as floating liquor stores.

While on Rum Row, McCoy's boats would post handwritten signs, showing the names and prices of his liquors. Each day, McCoy's customers, dozens at a time, drove their contact boats up to his vessels. They would keep their motors running while buying his much-revered liquor products. At the time, the small, quick contact boats were able to outrun Coast Guard ships and would then transfer their cargo to a bootlegger's waiting truck on the mainland.

Captain McCoy was popular for his fair prices, offers of free samples and a free case per order to regular paying customers. Within hours of his arrival, McCoy would sell his entire cargo. McCoy made one voyage a month, and during his career he offloaded over 175,000 cases of alcohol (mainly scotch and rye), making millions of dollars from selling his undiluted liquor.

Always the innovator, McCoy invented a convenient and safer way of moving and transporting liquor between vessels. Instead of using wooden cases, McCoy developed the smuggler's "ham" (a.k.a. "burlap sacks"). A ham was a large sack of six bottles stacked as a pyramid (stacked three, two, one) and wrapped tightly in straw and burlap. The hams were far lighter than wooden cases, and thus quicker and safer to transfer between vessels.

Photo of burlap sacks (a.k.a. "hams") that Bill McCoy invented and made famous. *Courtesy of the U.S. Coast Guard.*

McCoy had a number of friends, but none more loyal that his dog Old Faithful. McCoy and Old Faithful were inseparable. He even had a special bunk installed on the *Tomoka* since Old Faithful refused to sleep on the floor of the boat. One day, McCoy had to leave Old Faithful on the boat overnight since he had to go ashore for business. The next morning, McCoy found his dog sleeping right underneath the window of his hotel room. Old Faithful had swum ashore looking for his master.

On August 2, 1921, the *Henry L. Marshall* was seized off New Jersey by the U.S. Coast Guard cutter *Seneca*. The *Marshall* had been chartered to another rumrunner. After becoming drunk, the captain began to brag to an undercover agent about selling illegal liquor, setting the stage for the boat's capture. As the owner of the *Marshall*, McCoy was indicted. The *M.M. Gardner* and the *J.B. Young*, other McCoy vessels, were later seized

While on the run from law enforcement, one of McCoy's stops was in New London, Connecticut. He registered under an assumed name in a local hotel. While there, McCoy was informed that his crew from the *Arethusa* had removed five hundred cases of liquor from his vessel. So, while he was in New London, McCoy sold his liquor to residents there as well as to customers in other parts of Connecticut. But once he got word that the law enforcement men were closing in, McCoy fled to live in the Bahamas.

In 1923, after long negotiations, the United States reached a treaty agreement with Britain to push the Rum Line from three miles to twelve miles from shore. However, this was an agreement in principle, since the treaty was not signed that year. Allegedly, the twelve-mile limit was set based on a one-hour sail time from shore, and the previous three-mile limit was set by the distance of a cannon shot. (The old eighteenth-century cannons could fire no more than three miles.) The reasoning behind the twelve-mile limit was that it would make it harder for the smaller and less seaworthy boats to make the trip.

On November 23, 1923, the U.S. Coast Guard cutter *Seneca* received direct orders from the U.S. Department of Justice to capture Bill McCoy and the *Tomoka* (or, if necessary, sink the boat)—at all costs—even if in international waters. The State Department, the Department of Justice, the Prohibition agents and the U.S. Coast Guard all set their sights on capturing McCoy. To the government, McCoy was a symbol of defiance. Officials were determined to capture him at all costs. Bill McCoy was proclaimed Public Enemy Number 1 by the U.S. Coast Guard.

On Sunday, November 25, 1923, the *Tomoka* with Bill McCoy aboard was seized six and a half miles off the coast of Seabright, New Jersey—well beyond the three-mile Rum Line limit that McCoy thought he was abiding by. Once again, it was the U.S. Coast Guard cutter *Seneca* that was involved in the seizure of Bill McCoy's boat. A warning shot from one of the *Seneca*'s four powerful guns led to McCoy's surrender. The *Tomoka* was the first ship of British registry to be seized on rumrunning charges outside the three-mile limit. Bill McCoy, his skipper and seven members of the *Tomoka*'s crew were charged with illegally transporting liquor into the United States.

Great Britain protested, stating that the new twelve-mile treaty had not been signed. The British government was also upset that there were British and Canadian crewmen onboard the *Tomoka* when the vessel was seized.

Now the darling of the media, Bill McCoy had reached legendary status at the time of his capture. He had become an international sensation for his swashbuckling adventures. As he walked into the packed Newark, New Jersey courtroom, reporters stood shoulder to shoulder ready to record every word from the tall, well-dressed gentleman. When things settled down in the courtroom, the judge asked what defense McCoy planned to make at his upcoming trial. McCoy could have planned to mount a defense that the United States had unlawfully captured and seized both him and his boat in international waters, knowing that the twelve-mile Rum Line treaty between the United States and Britain had not been signed. He could have made the case that he was prepared to go to trial since he was well outside the three-mile limit and therefore never broke the law since he was in international waters

U.S. Coast Guard cutter *Seneca* displaying cannons, 1922. *Library of Congress.*

and the U.S. government had no legal authority to arrest him. Instead, much to the surprise of many in the courtroom, the soft-spoken McCoy pleaded guilty, not wanting a long, drawn-out trial. The statement he gave was brief: "I have no tale of woe to tell you. I was outside the three-mile limit, selling whiskey, and good whiskey, to anyone and everyone who wanted to buy. I'm an honest lawbreaker."

On April 21, 1924, Congress agreed to the twelve-mile Rum Line limit and agreed to make arrangements for the formal signing of the agreement. Ironically, the twelve-mile Rum Line limit which the United States supported would serve to only strengthen gangster control of bootlegging. The twelve-mile limit did make it more difficult for the smaller contact boats to make the trip. However, the mob had larger, more powerful boats, and this gave them almost free rein of the waterways.

In March 1925, despite Britain's protest of the seizure of the *Tomoka*, McCoy was sentenced to nine months in prison. Sadly, his best friend, Old Faithful, died while he was in jail.

McCoy was released from jail on Christmas Day 1925 to his brother Ben. McCoy moved to Florida and returned to the boatbuilding business and a

View from *Seneca* showing rumrunner with cases on deck. *Library of Congress*.

real-estate investment with Ben. On December 30, 1948, Bill McCoy died of a heart attack at age seventy-one in Stuart, Florida. He was at sea, where he was the happiest—aboard his private yacht *Blue Lagoon*.

Bill McCoy made a notable mark in maritime history. Aside from his law-breaking adventures, his high-quality liquor and his inventive seagoing techniques, Bill McCoy's bravery and compassion were well documented. Media reports at the time made note of the instances when he put his own life on the line to help those in need, including his enemies. The media recounted one circumstance when he went out of his way to get a Prohibition officer out of a jam. On another occasion, McCoy saved an entire hijacking crew from drowning—even after their unsuccessful attempt to pirate one of his boats. The hijackers' boat had become disabled, and the crew, freezing and wet, were left to die in the vast waterways. McCoy not only rescued the crew but also made sure they were properly fed while he and his men repaired their boat and let them go on their way without any retaliation.

By all accounts, Bill McCoy was, indeed, the "Real McCoy."

RUMRUNNER BOATS AND
NOTEWORTHY MARITIME INCIDENTS

The stakes were high, the payoff and cash were impressive. And yet, in honesty, the "game" was important. It was chess and checkers at sea, each involvin' so much skill and patience.

—*rumrunner for Nellie Green*

Rumrunning was the act of transporting (smuggling) illegal alcohol across the waterways and eventually into the hands of onshore bootleggers and other customers. The liquor that was illegally distributed included a wide variety of alcohol such as gin, whiskey, rum and wines.

While a great deal of risk was involved, many of the rumrunners were superb navigators who adeptly used their fast speedboats to outrun and outmaneuver the Coast Guard cutters. Many of these lawbreakers made a lucrative career out of rumrunning. However, like Bill McCoy and others, many rumrunners enjoyed the "thrill of the chase" as much (or more) than the money. As one of Nellie Green's rumrunners put it, the undertaking was "a fun and exciting cat and mouse game."

Rumrunner at night, 1924. *Library of Congress.*

Bill McCoy and his much-revered liquor proved to be a tough act to follow. Most of the rumrunners at sea did not sell the high-quality (expensive), uncut liquor to their customers that McCoy was famous for. Instead they would sell cut (diluted) liquor which increased the number of bottles to sell. They had full bottling and labeling operations onboard and filled "custom" orders from the bootleggers. To fill an order, the onboard crew provided the "phony" real brand labels, the "federal" seals, the "bonded" corks, added coloring to the alcohol (if requested) and then dipped the alcohol bottles in saltwater to give the bottles the "just off the boat" appearance. Onshore bootleggers and customers paid millions for the bootlegged whiskey, but rarely was the liquor ever again the quality of the Real McCoy.

During Prohibition, there were numerous rumrunner boats, each with its own story to tell. Several incidents involving the capture of rumrunners became legendary in maritime history during the Prohibition era. Some incidents caused an outcry by the American public, and several even created an international incident. Here are three examples.

THE *BLACK DUCK* INCIDENT

The tragic events surrounding the capture of the *Black Duck* caused a great public outcry in the United States. Rumrunners were used to nighttime sailing and the occasional inclement weather. Early Sunday morning, December 29, 1929, was no exception. A thick fog had settled in, challenging the navigational expertise of the crewmen on the New England rumrunner vessel known as the *Black Duck*. While sailing the waterways in the Narragansett Bay off the coast of Rhode Island, the vessel was spotted by the Coast Guard patrol boat CG-290. The Guardsmen received direct orders to open fire on the Black Duck. Three crewmen were shot and killed during this incident. After its capture, the *Black Duck* was escorted to the Coast Guard base in New London, Connecticut. This event did not go unnoticed by Americans, who were becoming more and more wary of all the violence and deaths caused by the enforcement of the Prohibition law. For many Americans, the *Black Duck* became a symbol of the failures of Prohibition. This unfortunate incident has been credited as one of the contributing factors for the shift in public opinion and the eventual repeal of the Prohibition Act.

The *Black Duck*, rumrunner. *Courtesy of the Boston Public Library, Leslie Jones Collection.*

THE SINKING OF THE *I'M ALONE*

The Nova Scotia rumrunner known as the *I'm Alone* transported illegal liquor mainly up and down the East Coast. On Friday, March 22, 1929, *I'm Alone* was fired on and sunk by the U.S. Coast Guard cutter *Dexter.* As a result of the shots fired, one of the *Dexter*'s crew members was killed.

The sinking of *I'm Alone* caused an international incident, with protests from Canada and Britain. The primary reason for the complaints was that the British-flagged (Canadian) schooner was attacked in international waters. The final report of an international investigation ordered the United States to make an official apology to the Canadian government and pay fines to Canada and the crew of the *I'm Alone.*

THE CAPTURE OF THE *TOMOKA*

As we have previously seen, Bill McCoy became an international sensation and gained the fascination of the American public with his well-documented adventures as the famed rumrunner and founder of Rum Row. The capture of his beloved *Tomoka* outside the three-mile Rum Line limit caused an international incident between the United States and Britain. While he could have presented a strong defense since he was technically in international waters when captured, McCoy pleaded guilty, not wanting a long, drawn-out trial. Even today, people from around the world marvel at the swashbuckling adventures of the "Real McCoy."

CONNECTICUT RUMRUNNER BOATS

Connecticut had its share of rumrunner boats transporting illegal alcohol along the East Coast and beyond. One such boat was the *Jenny T*, which was captured by law enforcement officers on Saturday, July 23, 1921. Eighteen men were arrested, and the *Jenny T* was seized in the vicinity of the pier at Lighthouse Point in New Haven, Connecticut. The *Jenny T* was carrying a large cargo of illegal alcohol, and crew members were charged with the "illegal transportation of intoxicating beverages."

Another Connecticut rumrunner vessel that received widespread media coverage was the *Scipio*. What follows is the story of the circumstances surrounding the capture and the tragic outcome of the *Scipio* and its crew.

THE *SCIPIO* INCIDENT

My name's Charlie—just Charlie.
—*engineer of the* Scipio *rumrunner*

The sixty-foot rumrunner boat known as the *Scipio* was the product of Bridgeport, Connecticut. The speedy *Scipio*, powered by three motors, was well known in many areas along the East Coast, especially Connecticut and Long Island. The vessel was a sister boat to the *Zip* and the *Whispering Winds*

Coast Guard cutter *Seneca* capturing a rumrunner, 1924. *Library of Congress*.

(also Bridgeport products). The *Whispering Winds* was seized by the Coast Guard with a cargo of five hundred cases of illegal liquor on June 18, 1931, near Plum Island (New York). The *Zip* was captured near Mattituck Inlet (New York) on April 7, 1932, carrying four hundred cases of whiskey.

On Wednesday, May 4, 1932, the *Scipio* was spotted by the U.S. Coast Guard sailing off Fisher's Island (Suffolk County, New York), less than two miles off the southeastern coast of Connecticut. A high-speed chase ensued, with the vessel speeding toward the Rum Line. During the pursuit, most of the rumrunning crew took shelter behind the sacks of liquor on the deck of the boat. The patrol boat fired several warning shots, which were ignored by the crew, so the pursuit continued. Finally, the patrol boat began rapid machine gun fire. Hundreds of shots were aimed at the *Scipio*, with one of the bullets hitting the vessel's engineer directly in the head. It was then that the crew surrendered to the Coast Guard. The engineer was rushed to the Lawrence and Memorial Hospital in New London, Connecticut.

The New London Coast Guard authorities found four hundred cases of liquor on the *Scipio*. In addition to the engineer, the crew consisted of men from Fairfield (Connecticut), Bridgeport (Connecticut) and New Bedford (Massachusetts). Coast Guard officials were unable to find any papers onboard the *Scipio*. The authorities believed that all documents were purposely destroyed to conceal details about the identities of the boat and crew.

Over five hundred bullets perforated the *Scipio*, including twenty-five bullets in the wheelhouse, twenty-five more in the hull and more than thirty around the boat's cabin. One Guardsman said that the *Scipio* resembled "swiss cheese."

The stricken engineer was known to his crew and to the authorities only by his first name. In a frantic effort to find out his true identity, the nurse treating him bent down closely and asked his name. In a faint whisper, the dying engineer responded, "My name's Charlie—just Charlie."

10

WOMEN BOOTLEGGERS

Women bootleggers resort to all sorts of tricks, concealing metal containers in their clothing….Their detection and arrest is far more difficult than that of male lawbreakers.
—*Georgia Hopley, first female Prohibition agent*

There were a number of other female bootleggers who possessed the same characteristics as Nellie Green—toughness, fearlessness, decisiveness, gutsiness, independent thinking and an ability to overcome tragedy. Here are a few of Nellie's counterparts in the bootlegging and rumrunning business during the Prohibition era.

GERTRUDE "CLEO" LYTHGOE

Perhaps the most popular and most respected female rumrunner during the Prohibition era was Gertrude "Cleo" Lythgoe (a.k.a. Grace Lythgoe). Her nickname "Cleo" was an homage to Cleopatra, the queen of Egypt. Cleo was an attractive, independent woman who was known for her keen business instincts and her no-nonsense, calculated approach to rumrunning. Qualities such as these enabled Cleo to become successful and wealthy. Cleo was born in Ohio and ran her rumrunning operations out of Bimini and Nassau (Bahamas). Cleo's beauty, brashness and charismatic life made her a media sensation. Always with her loaded pistol at her side, Cleo earned the respect of her fellow rumrunners, especially the legendary Bill McCoy, who founded Rum Row. On occasion, Cleo sailed aboard McCoy's schooner *Tomoka* to Rum Row, and the two, for a brief time, joined forces in the distribution of illegal whiskey. Cleo's last cargo run was in 1925, when she decided to quit the rumrunning business. Her expertise in the rumrunning trade earned Gertrude "Cleo" Lythgoe the titles "Queen of the Bahamas" and "Queen of Rum Row."

MARIE WAITE

Marie Waite (a.k.a. "Spanish Marie") picked up where Cleo Lythgoe left off. Marie entered the rumrunning and bootlegging business in 1926, and she single-handedly built a liquor empire. Her fleet consisted of four speedy vessels running liquor between Havana and Key West, Florida, plus fifteen speedboats to distribute cargo across Florida. Her rumrunning exploits during the Prohibition era have been said to have yielded her close to $1 million. Marie Waite's reign as a rumrunner extraordinaire ended abruptly on March 12, 1928, when she was captured by law enforcement along with her boat *Kid Boots*—with thousands of bottles of illegal liquor aboard.

GLORIA DE CASARES

Hailing from England, Gloria de Casares (born Mabel Davy) was a rumrunner married to a wealthy Argentinean. The British media called her "the beautiful rumrunner" and noted that she received many offers from movie producers to film her life story. Her boat *Gloria* was a five-masted ship and bore a resemblance to a pirate ship. She later rechristened her vessel the *General Serret*. Gloria's rumrunning career ended in 1925 when law enforcement apprehended her and seized the *General Serret* carrying a load of ten thousand cases of illegal scotch.

WILLIE CARTER SHARPE

It was the excitement that got me, outwitting the feds. Cars scattering, dashing along the streets.

—Willie Carter Sharpe

From 1926 to 1931, Willie Carter Sharpe of Roanoke, Virginia, conducted rumrunning activities on land. She was best known for piloting her automobile at extremely high speeds behind liquor caravans along the road from Franklin County to Roanoke. Her roadster pilot car was equipped with a special rear-end gadget (to fend off the feds) and steel fenders.

Willie acted as the driver of the "blocked car," the object being to foil pursuing officers by blocking their attempts to reach the liquor cars or to lead them off the trail in a mad dash over circuitous side roads while the main caravan continued to its destination. She would divert Prohibition officers by taking them on races, zigzagging over the torturous mountain roads and down the main streets of Roanoke and other towns. It was said that Willie would take dangerous hairpin turns at nearly eighty miles per hour.

From 1926 until she was apprehended in May 1931, Willie hauled more than 110 gallons on each run and a total of 220,000 gallons of illegal rum during that period of time.

With her teeth decorated with dazzling diamond insets, Willie was unapologetic when she was captured, saying, "It was the excitement that got me, outwitting the feds—Cars scattering, dashing along the streets."

Willie Carter Sharpe's daring exploits in piloting rum-filled automobiles from Franklin County to Roanoke are legend in Southwest Virginia.

JENNIE JUSTO

Jennie Justo, born Vinzenza DiGilormo, was an attractive young bootlegger. Jennie ran a speakeasy out of her home on Spring Street in Madison, Wisconsin. She sold illegal liquor, mainly to college students at the University of Wisconsin (all young adults) and earned enough money to put herself through school at the university. Jennie was arrested by the feds and sentenced to six months in prison at the Milwaukee House of Corrections.

When asked for a comment, Jennie Justo unapologetically defended her bootlegging activities, stating that "the only villains were the federal officials." Upon her release, Jennie received a warm reception from her loyal campus customers.

JOSEPHINE DOODY

Josephine Doody was a former dance hall girl who became a successful bootlegger. She was sixty-six years old when Prohibition began. She lived in a remote cabin in Glacier National Park, Montana. Her best customers were railroad men. A train would pull up near her homestead, and each toot of the horn indicated an order for one gallon of her homemade liquor. Josephine delivered her illegal booze in a small boat across the river, supplying the trainmen with the requested alcohol in the wilderness of Glacier National Park. Josephine Doody became known as the "Bootleg Lady of Glacier Park."

EDNA GIARD

Edna Giard was a Chicago bootlegger who (along with her husband) helped transport alcohol for Al Capone. Edna became friends with Capone's wife.

LAVINIA GILMAN

Lavinia Gilman of Butte, Montana, was an eighty-year-old matronly looking woman who was known to her family and friends as "Auntie Vine." Lavinia was also a very successful bootlegger, selling her homemade liquor from a three-hundred-gallon still. After her arrest, the judge refused to believe Lavinia was capable of such an illegal operation. Instead, the judge blamed her son for the illegal liquor transactions.

MARY ANN MORIARITY

Mary Ann Moriarity had a laundry business and washed clothes for residents in the area. She was also a bootlegger. When delivering her illegal liquor to her customers, Mary Ann would hide bottles of whiskey in baskets of clean laundry.

MARY WAZENIAK

Mary Wazeniak was a thirty-four-year-old Polish immigrant who lived in La Grange Park, Illinois. She operated a saloon out of her house. After drinking Mary's liquor, one of her customers died on the way home. The liquor was found to be tainted whiskey, and Mary Wazeniak was arrested. She was convicted and given an "indeterminate" sentence of one year to life for selling poisoned liquor. At her trial, the media referred to her as "Moonshine Mary."

BERTIE (BIRDIE) BROWN

Bertie (Birdie) Brown was a very well-known bootlegger operating out of her home in Fergus County, Montana. Her customers agreed that she had the best liquor in the area. Tragically, Bertie died from burns sustained when her still exploded in 1933.

STELLA BELOUMANT

Stella Beloumant was the leading bootlegger in Elko, Nevada. Her operations became so widespread that they drew the attention of a team of law enforcement officers that included the U.S. Attorney General, members of the Prohibition Bureau and the district attorney. Stella was finally caught as a result of a twenty-four-hour stakeout, and law officials hauled away a massive amount of illegal whiskey.

11

THE FLAPPER PHENOMENON AND "LIPSTICK"

He's the bees knees.

Flappers were smart and sophisticated, with an air of independence about them, and so casual about their looks and clothes and manners as to be almost slapdash. I don't know if I realized as soon as I began seeing them that they represented the wave of the future, but I do know I was drawn to them. I shared their restlessness, understood their determination to free themselves of the Victorian shackles of the pre-World War I era and find out for themselves what life was all about.
—Colleen Moore, famous flapper, actress

The "restlessness" that Colleen Moore was referring to can be traced back to World War I. During the war, many women took jobs outside their homes to support their families while scores of young men were fighting overseas. This was, indeed, a cultural change from prewar years when young women were confined to their homes, consigned to being content with keeping up with household chores. Conservative values dominated American social life up until the end of World War I. During these "Victorian" times, it was commonplace for young women to wait at home for young men to call on them and court them. However, the end of World War I saw nearly a whole generation of young men who had died or were severely wounded, leaving many young women without possible suitors. The horror of the war impressed on young women the feeling that life is short and can end at any moment. Instead of staying home waiting and preparing for a man who might never come, many young women decided that they were going to enjoy life—to its fullest.

It was also a time when women finally won the right to vote with the historic passage of the Nineteenth Amendment, which was ratified on August 26, 1920. In addition, the rise of the automobile was an important development. The automobile provided young girls (and boys) newfound independence and allowed young people to come and go as they pleased, traveling much longer distances than their parents ever dreamed. Finally, once the war was over, America experienced an economic boom, which meant that many young people now had purchasing power. The yearning for living life to its fullest coupled with their newfound freedoms gave rise to the new woman—more commonly known as the flapper.

Flappers were icons of the Roaring Twenties. They were a generation of young women who wore short skirts, spoke their own language, had their own fashion, wore their hair short in a bobbed cut, danced at nightclubs until late hours, frequented dance halls and speakeasies, listened and danced to jazz music and flaunted their disdain for Prohibition and for most of what was considered acceptable behavior at the time. Flappers challenged traditional Victorian roles, always pushing the boundaries. They no longer felt powerless and fully embraced consumerism and the freedom of personal choice. Flappers considered themselves equal in many ways to men of the era, especially in speakeasies.

In 1922, a new magazine was published to celebrate the flapper movement and took direct aim at those old-fashioned "fogies" who continued to embrace the prewar Victorian values and who openly rejected the new woman movement. The magazine was fittingly titled *The Flapper (Not for Old Fogies)*. The cover of the first issue of *The Flapper* magazine featured flapper icon Marie Prevost.

> *Pluck your eyebrows, roll your socks,*
> *Rouge your cheeks and bob your locks,*
> *Dab your nose and dress up swell,*
> *And tell the prudes to go to…*
> —*poem in the May 1922 edition of* The Flapper *magazine*

Movies also began to embrace the flapper movement and popularized the image of the fun-loving flapper. One such movie was titled *The Flapper* and starred former Ziegfeld girl Olive Thomas. Movies such as this served as an inspiration for the young women of this era and the movie stars became instant role models for the new woman.

Connecticut was home to a number of new women, including famous flappers such as Zelda Sayre Fitzgerald and Lois Long.

Zelda's husband (famed novelist F. Scott Fitzgerald) proudly proclaimed that Zelda was the "first American flapper." Zelda Sayre was named after the heroine of an obscure 1800s novel and was the daughter an Alabama Supreme Court justice. Francis Scott Fitzgerald was named after Francis Scott Key, the American credited for writing the national anthem, "The Star-Spangled Banner."

At the beginning of Prohibition (1920), Zelda and F. Scott Fitzgerald took up residence in Westport, Connecticut. He was twenty-three, and she was nineteen years old. At the time, they were referred to as the "King and Queen of the Jazz Age." The couple even honeymooned in Westport after their marriage on April 3, 1920, at New York City's St. Patrick's Cathedral.

From May through September 1920, the Fitzgerald couple rented a large colonial home on 244 Compo Road South in Westport (the first house that Zelda and F. Scott lived together in). It was in this house that F. Scott wrote a large portion of his second book, *The Beautiful and Damned*, following his successful debut novel, *This Side of Paradise*. Zelda spent a good portion of her day swimming at Westport's Compo Beach.

Adjacent to the Fitzgerald house lived a handsome, reclusive multimillionaire named F.E. Lewis. He owned a 175-acre estate, now the centerpiece of the Longshore Club Park. As a shortcut to Compo Beach, Zelda would cut through Lewis's property. It is purported that F. Scott fashioned Jay Gatsby after Lewis and that F. Scott's experiences in Westport may have served as inspirations when writing *The Great Gatsby*.

Zelda and F. Scott lived an extravagant lifestyle and hosted many lavish parties in Westport, attended by F.E. Lewis and many other very wealthy and famous guests. Zelda could often be seen racing her sports car along Westport's Boston Post Road. She even wrecked the Fitzgerald car by driving over a fire hydrant in town, perhaps after imbibing too much, as she and F. Scott were quite famous for.

> *All I want to be is very young always and very irresponsible and to feel that my life is my own—to live and be happy and die in my own way to please myself.*
>
> —*Zelda Sayre Fitzgerald*

Flappers were not without their critics, especially older women who were still protective of Victorian values. Many individuals looked harshly on the flapper movement and viewed flappers as brash and out of control for "antics" such as smoking cigarettes in public, wearing excessive makeup, drinking alcohol and flouting social and sexual norms. Flappers, with their "Garçonne look" (tomboyish fashion style), represented a new world order. Thus, they were considered by some to be a real threat to deeply held values and norms.

In 1920, noted British physician R. Murray Leslie, in a much bewildering lecture, referred to the flapper as "the social butterfly type…the frivolous, scantily-clad, jazzing flapper, irresponsible and undisciplined, to whom a dance, a new hat, or a man with a car, were of more importance than the fate of nations."

The Roaring Twenties saw hemlines on all women's clothing rising considerably, in comparison to the dress styles during the Victorian era. Some areas would hire "beach police" who patrolled the area with a measuring tape in hand. Their job was to measure the distance between the bottom of a woman's bathing suit and her knee. Too much bare skin could result in a heavy fine. When it became apparent that too many

A beach official checks the amount of thigh exposed by young ladies in their bathing suits, 1922. *Author's collection.*

women were ignoring these rules, it became a pointless endeavor and the practice was abandoned later in the 1920s.

Thus, the culture war pitting old versus new had begun, in large part due to the flapper movement.

The flapper stands as one of the most enduring and recognizable images of youth and the new woman in the 1920s. Decades later, many modern-day Americans view the flapper of the Roaring Twenties as something of a cultural heroine. They were young, defiant, fast-moving, fast-talking, fun-loving, reckless and rebellious. Flappers were young women who romped through the Roaring Twenties, enjoying their newfound freedoms, unashamed and unapologetic.

ORIGIN OF THE TERM *FLAPPER*

The exact origin of the slang term *flapper* appears to be somewhat elusive, and ever-changing. The word can be traced back to at least the 1800s and actually originated in the United Kingdom and Australia.

In 1864, London's *Wild-Fowler* publication defined a flapper as "a young wild duck, in the state of immaturity, partly fledged, and consequently unable to soar in the air or to fly any distance." Other British references at that time refer to flappers as teenage girls flapping about in a lively and enthusiastic manner. In 1900, Joseph Wright's English *Dialect Dictionary* defined the term *flapper* in a number of ways, including

◊ "To wander about aimlessly; to gad about."
◊ "She's just flappin' up and down an o' about naught."
◊ "A young giddy girl."
◊ "A woman or girl who does not settle down to her domestic duties but goes gaddin' about."
◊ "A young bird of any kind only just able to fly, a young wild duck."

By the turn of the twentieth century, many more comparisons were made between a teenage girl and a wild bird flapping about in a restless manner.

In a 1903 article in the *Telegraph* (Brisbane, Australia), a reference is made to a "Flapper's Dance" involving girls dancing with their hair down (as opposed to the Victorian updo hairstyle). In 1907, English actor George

Graves referred to flappers as "young girls with their hair still hanging down their backs." The young and handsome Crown Prince Friedrich Wilhelm of Germany was an idol of backfische, the German word for "teenage girls" or "flappers." He would often be seen dancing, signing autographs, kissing the hands of the backfische, all in an innocent manner. The flappers adored the crown prince, and he adored them.

Another widespread theory on the origin of the term *flapper* has to do with a brief fad in the early 1900s in which many young women wore rubber galoshes left open to flap when they walked. This theory has been disputed by some historians.

And so, the pre–World War I references of the wild duck flapping its wings aimlessly and in a restless manner appear to be the most fitting characteristics and images that came to embody the 1920s flapper.

Consider for a moment films you may have seen of flappers in the Roaring Twenties, flapping their arms and legs, wildly dancing the Charleston or the Black Bottom. The visual of the wild duck flapping its wings seems to be a fitting image. Don't you think?

LOIS LONG (A.K.A. LIPSTICK)

Will somebody do me a favor and get me home by eleven pm sometime? And see that nobody gives a party while I am catching up? I do so hate to miss anything.

—*Lipstick*

One of the most famous flappers during the 1920s was Connecticut native Lois Long. Lois was born on December 15, 1901, in Stamford, Connecticut and was the oldest of three children of Reverend Dr. William J. Long and Frances Bancroft Long. Long's father was the pastor of the First Congregational Church of Stamford. He received a bachelor's degree from Harvard in 1892 and a master's and doctorate degrees from Heidelberg University in Germany in 1897.

Long attended Stamford Public Elementary School and was a graduate of Stamford Public High School, class of 1918. She then enrolled at Vassar College, concentrating on English and French. Lois graduated from Vassar in 1922 with a bachelor's degree in English. At Vassar, Long was very involved in college activities. For example, she was a cast member

Lois Long yearbook photo, 1922. *Author's collection.*

and producer of a number of college theatrical performances, including *If I Were King*, *The Purple Mask* and *A Thousand Years Ago*. Long wrote a comprehensive review of Vassar dramatics that was published in the *Poughkeepsie Eagle* newspaper. Always whimsical, Long said in jest, "There is nothing like Art for keeping the complexion clear and the figure youthful"

In April 1920, Lois Long received a bit of notoriety when she was named one of the twenty-five prettiest girls at Vassar. Long was also chosen as a member of Vassar's historic Daisy Chain, a prestigious award presented to Vassar students for their "leadership skills, class spirit, and eagerness to volunteer their time."

Long was also one of four editors of Vassar's *The Vassarion*. She was honored in Vassar's yearbook, class of 1922, proclaiming, "Producer Long is one of the most fascinating, charming, and versatile of Directors."

It was at Vassar that Lois Long honed her dramatic writing skills, which she would put to good use later in her career as a famous and successful critic for several influential and prestigious publications. From Vassar, Long went directly to New York, working first as a copywriter at *Vogue* magazine and then as a staff writer and drama critic at *Vanity Fair*.

In 1925, the fledging magazine *The New Yorker* was facing a financial crisis and close to becoming extinct. Enter Lois Long. Immediately upon being hired. Long found fame and success. She was hired to write a column on New York nightlife. Specifically, Long was assigned to write about New York City speakeasies and nightclubs and their customers during the Prohibition era.

Using the pseudonym "Lipstick," Long chronicled her nightly escapades of drinking, dining and dancing in nightclubs and speakeasies throughout the city. For Long, properly reporting on the nightclub scene to the fullest extent meant staying up all night, excessive drinking and dancing with the speakeasy customers. It was not uncommon for Long to arrive at her *New Yorker* office at three or four o'clock in the morning, completely intoxicated and still in her evening dress. After her all-night carousing, she would sit at her desk and, after sobering up a bit, hastily and jubilantly detail her wild escapades at numerous nightclubs. Purportedly, there were times when Long could be seen at her desk stripped down to her slip in hot weather and she playfully roller-skated between desks in the office. A free spirit indeed!

In one of her first columns, Long took a swipe at Prohibition and the public officials who conducted raids on speakeasies. Such raids, in her opinion, only served to temporarily interrupt her "girlish drinking delights in barrooms." Prohibition, in Long's opinion was "foolish and unenforceable."

Long's *New Yorker* columns were witty, insightful and satirical. As a champion of the flapper movement, she and her columns offered women a glimpse of the glamorous flapper lifestyle in which they could enjoy many of the same freedoms and vices as men. Long became known as "Miss Jazz Age."

Speaking as a flapper herself, Long once remarked, "I like music, and informality, and gaiety." Long spoke freely of the decadence of the 1920s in a witty, satirical and self-assured manner. She seemed to sum up her own lifestyle: "Tomorrow we may die, so let's get drunk and make love."

Through Long's columns, young women who could not afford to go to nightclubs were now able to read about what it was like to be a young, single, liberated woman. Readers lived vicariously through Long, who chronicled her wild escapades dancing and drinking in the finest nightclubs in New York: "The nightclub banquettes were excellent substitutes for the psychiatrist's couch, less expensive and certainly more fun....We talked out our troubles. There wasn't much chance to sulk. There was a reckless atmosphere we responded to."

Readers loved her columns and waited anxiously to read about her new revelations of the clubs she frequented and her satirical comments about law enforcement agents she encountered: "The evening was spoiled by a good old-fashioned raid...where burly cops kick down the doors and women fall fainting on tables and strong men fall under them and waiters shriek and start throwing bottles out of windows."

Long became an instant celebrity throughout the country (especially with her fellow flappers), with her celebrated critiques: "Here I go plodding around, in my conscientious, girlish way, to all kinds of places at all hours of the night with escorts only reasonably adept at the art of bar-room fighting, and nothing ever happens to me."

Often, Long commented (in her much-acclaimed whimsical manner) on the daily lifestyles that she and other women led as they would hop from one nightclub to another: "You were thought to be good at holding your liquor in those days if you could make it to the ladies' room before throwing up. It was customary to give two dollars to the cabdriver if you threw up in his cab."

"Lipstick" (aka Lois Long) at the New Yorker. *Author's collection.*

As Long used the pseudonym "Lipstick," readers had no idea who she was or what she looked like. In typical Lois Long fashion, she jokingly referred to herself in her columns as a "short squat maiden of forty." So, you can imagine the reaction of her fans when her attractive photograph was published upon the announcement of her marriage to *The New Yorker* cartoonist Peter Arno. Long and Arno were married by her father at her parents' home in Stamford, Connecticut, on August 13, 1927.

Thus, in Lois Long were combined two rare ingredients: an ability to be perpetually stimulated, blended with an ability to be perpetually critical.

OTHER FAMOUS FLAPPERS

Marie Prevost

Canadian-born Marie Prevost (real name Marie Bickford Dunn) was a popular actress who transitioned from silent films to talkies. She portrayed a flapper in a number of her movies. Prevost was featured on the front cover of the first issue of *The Flapper* magazine, merrily walking her pet duck (an apparent reference to the probable genesis of the term *flapper*—"a wild duck flapping its wings").

Colleen Moore

Colleen Moore was one of the earliest actresses to portray a lighthearted happy-go-lucky flapper girl in films. Colleen popularized the "bobbed" haircut.

Coco Chanel

Fashion designer Coco Chanel introduced the loose short dress that enabled flappers the freedom of movement, especially for "wild" jazz dances. One example is the Charleston, in which the dancers flap their arms and kick up their heels.

Left: The *Flapper Magazine*, featuring flapper Marie Prevost. *Author's collection.*

Right: Colleen Moore. *Library of Congress.*

Zelda Sayre Fitzgerald

Zelda Sayre Fitzgerald was dubbed the "first American Flapper" by her husband (F. Scott Fitzgerald). The couple were notorious partygoers and extremely popular with both fans and the media. Zelda and F. Scott Fitzgerald were former Connecticut residents, having lived, worked and partied in Westport.

Gilda Gray

Gilda Gray was dubbed the "Shimmy Queen" for popularizing the shimmy dance style, a trendy dance among many flappers. The shimmy was even immortalized years later in such popular songs as "Shimmy Like Kate" (by the Olympics), "Shimmy Shimmy Ko-Ko Bop" (by Little Anthony and the Imperials) and "Shimmy Shimmy" (by Bobby Freeman).

Clara Bow

Clara Gordon Bow received the nickname the "It Girl" after she achieved worldwide fame for her role in the silent movie *It*. Bow was extremely photogenic and the envy of many young women in the Roaring Twenties who felt she had "it."

> *We had individuality. We did as we pleased. We stayed up late. We dressed the way we wanted. I used to whiz down Sunset Boulevard in my open Kissel motor car. Today, they're sensible and end up with better health. But we had more fun.*
>
> —*Clara Bow, the "It Girl," flapper*

Norma Talmadge

According to the Talmadge/Green family, Norma Marie Talmadge and her sister Constance Talmadge were related to William Talmadge, husband of bootlegger Nellie Green. Norma Talmadge was one of the most elegant and glamorous film stars of the Roaring Twenties. She is considered one of the biggest silent film stars, ranking among the most popular actresses in the early 1920s. Norma was also a very successful film producer of the silent era. On October 20, 1917, Norma married her first husband (producer Joseph M. Schenck) in Stamford, Connecticut. Talmadge acted in several movies set in Connecticut locations such as Roxbury.

Constance Talmadge

Constance Talmadge was the younger sister of Norma Talmadge and one of silent pictures' most popular and enduring stars of the flapper era in the movie industry. As previously mentioned, according to the Talmadge/Green family, Constance and Norma were related to William Talmadge, husband of bootlegger Nellie Green. While her sister Norma concentrated on melodrama, Constance concentrated on romantic comedy. Her nicknames included: "Dutch," "Connie" and the "Vitagraph Tomboy."

Left: Norma Talmadge. *Right*: Constance Talmadge. *Library of Congress.*

Anita Page

Born Anita Evelyn Pomares, Anita Page made an easy transition from silent films to talkies. Her roles included the portrayal of a fun-loving girl, sometimes hard-drinking, sometimes flirtatious—the epitome of the flapper "jazz baby."

Norma Shearer

Norma Shearer was born Edith Norma Shearer. When she was eighteen years old, Shearer appeared (uncredited) in the 1920 movie *The Flapper*. She starred in dozens of films in the 1920s and thereafter. Nicknamed "Queen Norma," Shearer received six Academy Award nominations and earned another nickname, the "First Lady of MGM," for her success at MGM studios.

Louise Brooks

Louise Brooks, born Mary Louise Brooks, was a flapper sex symbol of the Roaring Twenties. Brooks popularized the iconic "bobbed" hairstyle,

The flapper look. *Author's collection.*

a style that would become emblematic of the 1920s flapper. Nicknames for Louise Brooks included the "Girl in the Black Helmet," "Lulu" and "Brooksie."

12

HOTEL TALMADGE

I'm gonna build a hotel, a great big one, and we won't sell rum by the glass,
we'll bring it in by the boatload.
—Nellie Green

Like so many of her other impromptu decisions, Nellie's idea of building the Hotel Talmadge came about as the result of a physical and verbal altercation.

Nellie's grandfather John and her father, Charles, were licensed to sell rum at the Dyke House Inn. However, after the sudden death of her first husband, Charles Hinckley, Nellie and her father let the license expire.

> *I jest didn't bother about it after my first husband passed. The Commissioner was always good to me. Fact is, he said to me "To hell with the license, you go and sell all the rum you want, we won't bother you." My original idea was to fix up the big grey barn in the back of Dyke House, where we used to fight chickens. We would have rooms on top and sell beer and rum downstairs. Even though the Commissioner said I didn't need a license, I figured I'd get one jest the same, to be legitimate. So, I went through the entire process of gettin' a license, notifying the public and gettin' their support, and getting' the best people to sign for me, all right and proper. All of a sudden I get approached by this fella from Branford with a petition in his hand to try to stop me, sayin' he didn't want no saloon goin' up. I tole him I did eveythin' legal like and I owned all this property. I tole him nicely to remove himself and go back to his own business. And, oh by the way mista', this is East Haven not Branford.*

Nellie continued,

> *But he wouldn't leave and begins verbally threatenin' Will and me, with bad stuff. I tole him he was trespassin' but he continued his threats. My Will, he wasn't much for takin' things in his own hands, but he decided he had enough of the threats. So, Will got me into his truck, drives down to this fella's business and proceeds to crash into the fella's barn. The man then makes the mistake of going after Talmadge, so Will hits him so hard the guy spun around and made a little whirlpool with his feet.*

But Nellie wasn't finished getting her point across to this person who began threatening both Will and her:

> *And so, right that second I got the idea—the idea of buildin' a hotel. So, when this no-account bum comes back to try to try to hurt my Will, I tell the guy "Here's what I'm gonna do. I'm tellin' you now. I'm gonna build a hotel, a great big one, and we won't sell rum by the glass, we'll bring it in by the boatload." That will fix ya!*

This incident occurred in 1901. Little did Nellie know that years later when she began her bootlegging adventure, her prophetic statement would become a reality. "So, I tell Will to hitch up the wagon, we were going to buy the lumber that very afternoon. And that was the start of it—the start of the Hotel Talmadge."

And so, the Dyke House was uprooted in 1901 and joined by a raised walkway to the large, spacious building that became known as the Hotel Talmadge. Nellie, Will and their newborn son, Charlie, stayed at the "ol' homestead" since it was still in working condition. Construction on Hotel Talmadge began in 1901 and was completed in 1902 to the delight of their ever-growing number of patrons. The cost of the hotel construction was $75,000. While the hotel was being built, Will became involved in another large construction project, a separate building in back of the hotel and on the south side of Snake Hill Road, called the Driftwood.

When the Hotel Talmadge was built, it accommodated nearly five hundred guests in the main dining room and large ballroom dance hall and a private dining room on the first floor. There were thirteen bedrooms on the second floor, with a bath at each end of the hall and seven bedrooms and two baths on the third floor. A separate suite was constructed for Nellie and Will. The hotel was known for its long, curving bar, accommodating many

Hotel Talmadge Hotel, 1902.

thirsty customers. Presiding behind the Hotel Talmadge bar was "Old Iron Horse Nellie," which came to be one of her nicknames.

Unlike other establishments of this kind, Nellie set down some strict rules, and God help the person who violated any one of them. From the outset, Nellie managed what she considered "a decent and respectable place." In Nellie's hotel, foul language and vulgarity were prohibited. And, unlike many other hotel owners, Nellie discouraged excessive liquor indulgence. As Nellie was known to tell customers who had one drink too many, "Comes a time when the man needs to go home to his family where he belongs." Also, women were not allowed to smoke in public, and carousing (especially infidelity) was forbidden by Nellie. To highlight this, Nellie recalled when a hotel guest once asked her, "Where's the girls?" Mincing no words, Nellie shot back, "You bastard, there ain't nawthin' like that aroun' here. There never was, and they ain't never goin' to be as long as I'm in charge. And whoever tole you anythin' like that is a damned liar. And the sooner you find out the better it will be for your stinkin' hide—before I skin you! You think you're smart. You're only smart when the skin's off!"

Being on the Farm River, just a half mile from Long Island Sound but not too close to the bright lights and scrutiny of large cities like New Haven, the Hotel Talmadge was ideally situated during Prohibition to secretly land the rumrunner boats carrying their illegal cargo. The hotel stairway leading to the caves was put to good use. Cases of booze would be silently unloaded from the cargo boats and stashed under the hotel, until it was time to distribute the illegal liquor.

During Prohibition, the Hotel Talmage became the hotspot for people of all persuasions—actors, actresses, politicians and businesspeople would

Nellie's Driftwood house.

all frequent Hotel Talmage for a night of entertainment and to joyfully imbibe in the various kinds of liquor that was sold there. Dance shows featuring large orchestras, and fancy dancing would provide customers musical enjoyment on the large ballroom floor.

Unlike some of the smaller speakeasies in New York City, no secret codes or passwords were necessary. After all, many of the politicians and local law enforcement officers at the time were not only frequent patrons of the inn but actually contributed (privately) to the creation of the hotel. For a time, Nellie also hired a former high-ranking law enforcement official as her hotel manager. That's not to say that the hotel was always off-limits for law enforcement raids. Indeed, Nellie's hotel was targeted for raids on a number of occasions, but Nellie managed to move her illegal liquor before the police arrived, many times having the luxury of advanced notification by "a regular and loyal customer" at the precinct.

And so, it was there at the foot of Snake Hill in East Haven, jutting out over the famed Farm River, that the Hotel Talmage would become "ground zero" for Nellie's bootlegging activities. It would be the site of many dramatic events, both lawful and unlawful. Sometimes rowdy, sometimes sad, sometimes funny, sometimes fabulous and often entertaining. It was, after all, the tumultuous Roaring Twenties.

Bunny Horton (*left*), restaurant manager, and Betty Talmadge, hotel operations manager.

Bunny Horton (restaurant manager) behind the bar.

Get together of family and friends at Hotel Talmadge. Charlie (in white outfit with tie) and his father, William, are seated in the front.

Hotel Talmadge.

Nellie was always "hands on" at Hotel Talmadge, even in her retirement.

Testimonial dinner for a former hotel manager (and former high-ranking law enforcement official).

Santa Claus visited Nellie Green's properties in East Haven as part of their many charitable events for the local residents.

Hotel Talmadge, 1970s.

With the repeal of Prohibition in December 1933, Nellie Green, now sixty years old, was once again a legitimate businesswoman and able to capitalize openly on her widely recognized rumrunning reputation, a reputation that extended well beyond Connecticut's borders. Though the country was by then in the grips of the Great Depression, the hotel establishment continued to thrive as a legitimate, upscale retreat. The hotel, commonly referred to as "Nellie Green's," became a famous nightclub, especially for the show biz crowd. Among the big-name stars that came out for the entertainment, often for weeks at a time, were John Barrymore, Bing Crosby, famed author Jack London, Rudy Vallée and Tyrone Power. A centenarian, known to family and friends as "Skippy," recalled meeting Tyrone Power at one time. "He was very attractive and very kind to me. He was wearing a gorgeous camel hair sports jacket and was accompanied by a lovely French woman."

But there was a part of Nellie Green that yearned for her days as a bootlegger. Despite all the challenges and all the risks involved in bootlegging, Nellie, by her own admission, missed the excitement that was an integral part of her life during the Prohibition era. This was the same sentiment that was expressed by some of her fellow bootleggers and rumrunners such as Bill McCoy, Cleo Lythgoe, Spanish Marie Waite and Gloria de Casares. For many bootleggers and rumrunners, the thrill of the chase was actually more exciting and rewarding than the vast profits they received.

To fill this excitement gap, Nellie turned to other things to motivate her interest. Showing her agility and playfulness, Nellie, at age sixty-six, would go surfboard riding on the same river where she had all those exciting and sometimes tragic experiences. As Nellie put it, "Ridin' them surf boards ain't nawthin' if you can keep your balance." She also spent a good deal of time tending to her horses. While her childhood horses Kit and Tom had long since passed, Royal Flush was still alive and well and treated to a royal life on Nellie's premises. The untimely death of her only son when she was sixty-nine caused Nellie to begin to lose interest in the operation of the hotel. By the early 1940s, Nellie, now in her seventies, had retired. Her daughter-in-law, Betty Talmadge, oversaw the operations of the hotel. Bunny Horton, a friend of Charlie's, served as restaurant manager. The Hotel Talmadge remained operational until the 1970s. The original building was eventually converted to condominiums.

But the "spirit" of Nellie Green lives on within the walls of the large establishment that still stands and also in the acres of land surrounding the building where Nellie spent her remarkable life.

13

NELLIE'S VIEWPOINT

I always had the feelin' that I'd never get away from the Farm River and the Rum.
—Nellie Green

A year before she passed away, Nellie Green shared her attitude toward life—whether it was bootlegging or life in general. Some of her rationale may be difficult for the average person to comprehend. But, right or wrong, she was sincere in her beliefs and didn't hold back.

> *I ain't never done nawthin' wrong in my life. They ain't got nawthin' on me. I don't care what people say about me as long as they don't attack my character.*

This is a very telling quote from Nellie and requires some explanation in terms of how she viewed her life and career.

Take, for instance, her statement "I ain't never done nawthin' wrong in my life." Here, Nellie is referring to her bootlegging career. Life circumstances prevented her from achieving the formal education that her mother had hoped for her. But, by all accounts, Nellie was an astute person, especially in business matters. So, it would stand to reason that Nellie knew full well that she was breaking the Prohibition law when she went into the bootlegging business. But, in Nellie's view, the Eighteenth Amendment was a foolish, unenforceable law that actually had an adverse effect on people's lives. In her opinion, otherwise law-abiding citizens were going to find a way to

Nellie Green Talmadge (at seventy-seven) with onlookers on the Farm River Bridge.

have a drink or two, despite the ban on liquor sales. Nellie believed that before people criticized her for her "unethical" bootlegging activities, they should first look at themselves. In her own life, she witnessed firsthand the cooperative, tolerant and laissez-faire attitude of the federal, state and local authorities who turned their back on the enforcement of the Prohibition law. This also went for politicians.

In her mind, Prohibition was a senseless law that should be ignored. After all, even her own native state of Connecticut declined to ratify the law. She always thought it was foolish of the government to not allow her to sell liquor (and therefore lose out on the tax revenue from liquor sales) and then naively fail to think that many individuals would take full advantage of this action. Others would gladly take matters into their own hands to serve the demands of so many people. In her opinion, it was a law that was not thought out well and had unintended consequences both for the public and for bootleggers like her. Prohibition was a financial bonanza for Nellie, and she enthusiastically made a fortune due to the liquor ban. Nellie conducted her bootlegging activities in a "fair" and "unapologetic" manner.

At an early age, Sugar was indoctrinated by her father's words and deeds that morality cannot be legislated. It was drilled into her mind. This applied to gambling on roosters, prize fights and horses. And when she was forty-seven years old, it applied to bootlegging liquor. Nellie was providing a service to a demanding public in a "clean, decent and respectable" establishment and, therefore in her mind, legitimate. The objection or "intervention" of law authorities was needless and unwarranted, and it actually worked against its intended purpose.

There appears to have been a common thread among many of the respected bootleggers and rumrunners at the time with regards to their view of the Eighteenth Amendment. Like Nellie Green, many other bootleggers felt that the Prohibition law was not serving its intended purpose and, therefore, should be ignored. Take for instance the famed rumrunner Bill McCoy, who admitted that he violated the Prohibition law. But, in his view, Americans have always "kicked holes in the laws they resented." Nellie Green broke the law and so did Bill McCoy. But McCoy famously called himself an "honest lawbreaker." Nellie Green, like McCoy, also truly felt that she broke the law in a justifiable and "honorable" way. And Nellie showed the same characteristics as her fellow woman bootleggers and rumrunners. Like Cleo Lythgoe and Willie Carter Sharpe, Nellie was an independent woman who conducted her activities in a fearless, no-nonsense manner and with a keen business sense.

What Nellie meant by "character" also takes some explanation. "Character" to Nellie meant that she had an unconditional loyalty to those who she believed were her friends (as we saw previously by her reaction to negative comments said about her close friend Ella Wheeler Wilcox). Character also meant that she was never delinquent on money owed to the local, state or federal government. And, as noted previously, Nellie could have easily taken advantage of King Tut and his money. She could have simply withdrawn all his money out of the bank, which he agreed to deposit in her name. But she had no intention of doing such a thing. She also agreed to pay all the tax due from the money deposited in the bank from their transactions—and did not ask King Tut to contribute to the tax payment. Nellie was widely known for her generosity shown to her friends and neighbors, many times in the form of private donations. Also, as we have seen, Nellie risked her own life to save numerous people from certain death in the Farm River.

Furthermore, character also meant her steadfast love of her family. Indeed, we saw this with her unconditional love of her only child, Charlie, especially when he became ill. She devoted an inordinate amount of time and depleted just about all her substantial wealth in caring for her loving son. So, too, was her devotion to family and friends who died before her. In her declining years, Nellie was obsessive in caring for the graves of those who had preceded her and of those who would follow her. When her beloved dog Patsy died, he was given an extravagant burial. And then there's Royal Flush, Nellie's beautiful and once famous show horse that was still happily grazing on her property. According to Nellie, arrangements had already been made for a lavish burial, with honors suited for royalty. Also, her son Charlie's 1936 Buick was still kept on her premises. As Nellie said, "It was Charlie's car. It stays his car. That's it."

And so, despite her outgoing, tough demeanor, Nellie Green had a heart of gold—and was not afraid to share her love with the people and things she treasured in her life.

But there was another side of Nellie's character—her sometimes puzzling violent nature and her flaunting of the law. To understand this other aspect of Nellie's character, it would probably help to consider the upbringing that Sugar was exposed to and had to deal with on a daily basis by her domineering father. While it is true that she was raised by her father in a rough and sometimes violent manner, she both loved and respected her father. Also, Nellie understood that her father's irrational behavior at times was a direct result of his Civil War injuries. It could be said that her "Papa" was the only man Nellie ever feared and the only person she felt was her "boss": "My father was the only one whoever dictated to me—the only one. My husbands never did. I had a lot of respect for both of my husbands, and I treated them very nice. But my father was my boss—even after I was married."

From the very beginning, Nellie's father ingrained in her that she must never walk away from a potential altercation when she felt she was verbally or physically threatened. Her fists were her answer. And her ability to physically handle herself sent fear through the hearts of even the most hardened men at the time. It was just as her father had planned when Sugar was a mere ten-year-old child—to use her fists to take care of "all comers." In a moment of reflection about her father's influence on her, Nellie was reminded of an old proverb her mother taught her: "As the twig is bent, so is the tree inclined." (In other words, the effect of a parent's influence on a young child's molding mind can shape who they are and how they act later in life.) Nellie firmly believed that she never violated any of the tenets of her self-imposed, self-fashioned code of personal morality. Right or wrong, she was the law unto herself.

On one occasion, a local policeman informed Nellie (in a kidding fashion) that a new law was just passed that banned people from using their fists to defend themselves. Nellie was taken aback and truly surprised. The reason she may have been surprised can be explained by her upbringing, in which the use of her fists and other physical ways to defend herself in any situation was justified—and no law, in her mind, could prevent her from doing so.

When using her physical force, Nellie didn't really analyze the right or wrong of her actions. She just "corrected" the situation, usually with her fists. Even when doing something in jest, Nellie didn't always think about the ramifications. Take, for instance, an incident with her longtime friend "Pop," who had worked for Will and Nellie for many years and was nearing seventy years old. By her own admission, Nellie was very much overweight. Pop once kidded Nellie that she was too "fat" to lift her feet. Nellie responded, in a playful manner, "You jest turn your back and see whether I'm too fat to lift my feet!" Not knowing what she was up to, Pop played along and turned around. Nellie proceeded to forcefully kick Pop into the water. While some of their friends found it amusing, others were a bit horrified since Pop hit the water head-first. Nellie proudly recalled, "Pop went head over heels. His behind was in a sling for a week." But Nellie never gave a thought that her actions could have resulted in Pop receiving a serious neck or back injury. To Nellie, it was just clean fun.

Nellie's statement, "They ain't got nawthin' on me," meant that almost everybody in the surrounding areas knew what she did and why she did it—and that she held nothing back.

Nellie always felt that if she ran her bootlegging business properly there would be no need for her to get mixed up with bribery or blackmail. As a rule, Nellie always tried to conduct her business in a straightforward manner—having been supported by her neighbors and "all those big shots in town." Nellie said, with emphasis,

I want this decidedly understood. Whenever someone made a complaint about me they—the state cops—they always came and done their duty. They arrested me if they had the chance. They never held back when they had a duty to perform. There was nawthin' between them and me which could have persuaded 'em when there was a formal complaint. If there was anythin' on their side, they got it. If there was anythin' on my side, I got it—the lack of

"Pop" (George Libby Sr.) and his longtime friend Nellie Green.

evidence, for example. But many's the time they went on a wild goose chase! I fought 'em the same way they fought me, and we were friends. And if they didn't get nawthin' on me—well, that was all right, too.

Nellie was brought up with the moral code of "You scratch my back and I'll scratch yours." This was evident when she agreed to have the Farm River bridge destroyed. The Trap Rock Quarry owner agreed to help fix up the rear of the Dyke House if Nellie agreed to have the outdated Farm River bridge destroyed. He had done her a favor. She returned the favor. Simple as that.

So, what unethical behavior bothered Nellie in her hotel operations? To begin with, liquor overindulgence was a concern. Unlike many other speakeasy hotel operators, Nellie's ethical code on certain behavior was strict and not debatable. Instead of turning her back (or even encouraging) a nearly intoxicated man to have that extra drink, Nellie would tell the individual to immediately leave her premises. Excessive indulgence was troubling to Nellie, especially, as she put it, "when the offendin' individual has cashed his pay-check and is spendin' money which don't belong to him but to his family, and he ought to go home in the first place." She did not allow her customers to use vulgarity and banned "off-color" jokes in her establishment. She did confess to using a "mild" form of profanity but only when provoked. Nellie also banned discussions about politics and religion in her hotel, as they almost certainly would result in provocations and altercations.

"Unaccepted familiarity" by strangers (drunk or sober) was not accepted in her hotel. Women who were outwardly unfaithful to their husbands or any attempt by "an ole bag" to sneak up the stairs of the Hotel Talmadge would incur Nellie's wrath and be thrown out of her establishment—physically, if needed. This applied to even her own friends and acquaintances who frequented her hotel. This being said, Nellie tended to be completely indifferent once people left her establishments. "That's their business. It doesn't interfere with mine, it doesn't involve me in no way."

At age seventy-seven, Nellie was still very alert and still feisty. But by this time, she was slowed down considerably by a severe heart problem. The events in and around Farm River had taken their toll on Nellie. Until the day she died, her superstition concerning the Farm River's dominance had haunted her. There were many times that she cursed the river, holding it responsible for, among other things, her son's untimely death. For Nellie, the river represented all that she could not escape. She had thought that she could escape life on the Farm River through her singing career, only to have it abruptly cut short when she felt obliged to take care of her ailing mother. She also had hopes and dreams of moving the family to Pennsylvania once her son became a corporate lawyer, only to have that dream dashed by life's tragedies.

In her declining years, Nellie resigned herself to living out the rest of her life on Farm River: "This is the God damnedest place I have ever known. To me, there ain't nawthin' like it on the planet. You can get mad with every change of the tide. Sometimes I think there was no escapin' this damn river and its effect on my life. No escapin' at all."

The word *nemesis* comes to mind. Whether based on fact or on superstition, for Nellie Green, both the Farm River and her father were her true nemeses.

She also reminisced about her combative nature, the product of her rough upbringing. Nellie admitted that, while some people might consider it violent, it did make her blood flow "Sometimes it made me feel good. What's that stuff that runs through your veins when you get riled?" Nellie never lost her fighting spirit and remained unapologetic in her use of her fists or other physical force over the years when the situation called for it. But this, too, managed to wear her down.

The Talmadge family standing in front of car and dog Patsy.

Months before she died, Nellie, in a reflective moment and in a submissive way, uttered a well-known Shakespearean quote as a way of surrendering to her lifelong combative nature: "I'm afraid that my head was always as full of quarrels as an egg is full of meat."

This was actually a powerful and profound statement by Nellie Green. She must have learned this expression from her mother, whom Nellie proudly referred to as "well-learned and a reader of all things." The quote is from Shakespeare's *Romeo and Juliet*, when, after the couple marry, hot-headed Mercutio (itching for a fight with the rivaling Capulets), taunts Romeo's cousin Benvolio: "Thy head is as full of quarrels as an egg is full of meat [yolk]; and yet thy head hath been beaten as addle as an egg for quarreling." To say it another way, "Your head is as full of quarrels as an egg if full of yolk—and yet you have been hit so many times for picking fights that your brains are now as scrambled as an egg."

There never seemed to be a consistent period of serenity in Nellie's life. However, in the years prior to her death, Nellie was buoyed by the constant stream of visitors who came to see her in East Haven. Her friends would come in from all over the country to visit and reminisce. Nellie would share both light-hearted and sad moments that were such an integral part of her life. Her Washington friends shared stories of

Nellie in back seat of the car, husband William standing next to the car, Charlie in front seat, Charlie's sons Charles II (with foot up) and William II sitting.

Family and friends pose for a photo at the Hotel Talmadge.

Nellie Green holding a portrait of herself in her younger days that appeared in an extensive newspaper article.

Left: Nellie Green Talmadge at age seventy-seven.

Below: The Green-Talmadge grave site in East Haven's East Lawn Cemetery. *Author's collection.*

The legendary Nellie Green.

Nellie's many singing engagements there. Writers and artists reminisced with Nellie about their common interests and experiences with Ella Wheeler Wilcox. Actors, critics and friends delighted in her amusing stories of the Hotel Talmadge at its height. To their amazement, Nellie even shared certain tales of her bootlegging adventures (in a general sense, without naming names). Nellie very much looked forward to these visits, especially in her later years.

Nellie's husband, Will, died of a heart attack in January 1950, just four months shy of their fiftieth wedding anniversary. Nellie would soon follow her husband.

For seventy-eight years, Nellie lived a very tumultuous life. It was a life filled with excitement, adventure, anguish, tragedy, violence and heartbreak. But, through it all, Nellie retained her dignity, honesty, self-assurance and (at times) a childlike curiosity.

On October 14, 1951, Nellie Green died. Her family and friends were there at her side. Nellie's death and biography were covered in printed media throughout the United States. Local newspapers such as the *New Haven Journal-Courier* and the *New Haven Evening Register* paid front-page homage to a "Connecticut Legend." Nellie Green was, indeed, a living legend and a folk hero to many in Connecticut and surrounding areas.

Nellie's traditional Irish wake was held at the W.S. Clancy Funeral Home in Branford, Connecticut. Two days later, with the temperature at a warm seventy degrees, Nellie was buried between her beloved husband, Will, and son, Charlie, in the Green-Talmadge plot in East Haven's East Lawn Cemetery. A two-foot-high tombstone marks her final resting spot.

"Sugar" is finally at peace.

NICKNAMES OF RUMRUNNERS, PROHIBITION AND MORE

AIRDALE | a lookout, especially one who signaled rumrunners when the coast was clear

BANANA BOATS (BANANA FLEET) | streamlined, low-slung boats designed for rumrunning

BLIND PIG | an illegal saloon

BLOCKADE | a line of watercraft deployed to close a port, harbor, or section of coast to prevent liquor smugglers from entering or leaving

BOTTLE FISHERMAN | a commercial fisherman who quit fishing and joined the ranks of the rumrunners.

COASTIES | U.S. Coast Guard personnel

CONTACT BOAT | (a.k.a. blockade runner, daughter boat, fireboat, distributor, feeder boat, in-between boat, rum lugger, shore runner, mosquito boat) | a small fast vessel, especially a speedboat, which picked up liquor from a mother ship and transported it to shore.

CUTTERIZED | rumrunner slang for being followed by a Coast Guard cutter

DOCK FIXER | the person who supervised the unloading of illegal liquor and bribed officials to ensure that law enforcement didn't interfere

DRY FLEET OR DRY NAVY | the vessels and personnel of the U.S. Coast Guard and other government entities that enforced Prohibition on the waterways

FIREMEN | the crew on a fireboat (contact boat)

FIREWATER | alcohol or intoxicating beverages

GO-THRU-GUYS | hijackers

HAM (a.k.a. BURLAP SACK) | a large sack, usually burlap, filled with bottles of liquor surrounded by straw or another cushioning material, invented by famed rumrunner Bill McCoy

HIJACK (a.k.a. KNOCK OFF A LOAD) | to steal a cargo in transit; to illegally seize control of a vessel.

HOOLIGANS' NAVY | rumrunners' nickname for the U.S. Coast Guard

ISLE OF RUM | the Bahamas

JOHNNIE WALKER'S NAVY | the rumrunning fleet, especially the vessels on Rum Row

LAND SHARK | a bootlegger who picked up liquor from a boat on the beach or at the dock

MONK OR MONKEY (a.k.a. SWAMPER) | a rumrunners' underling who did menial chores, such as loading liquor on the boat

MOTHERSHIP (a.k.a. PARENT SHIP) | a large watercraft carrying a cargo of liquor that would be sold to smaller vessels.

NO MAN'S LAND | Rum Row.

OVER THE RAIL OR OVER THE SIDE | transferring liquor from one watercraft to another on the high seas without putting into port

PILOT CAR | an automobile leading a convoy of trucks or cars carrying illegal liquor

PROHIBITION PIRATE (a.k.a. booze buccaneer, rummer, moonlighter) | a rumrunner

PROHIS | nickname for Prohibition agents and the federal agency that enforced the Volstead Act

RUM CHASER | A Coast Guard ship or another law enforcement vessel that pursued rumrunners

RUM LINE | the border that separated U.S. territorial waters from international waters during Prohibition

RUNNING DARK | sailing without lights

SCOTCH NAVY | a fleet of rumrunning vessels, especially the motherships on Rum Row

WATER SHARK | a contact boat skipper or crewman

WHISKITO FLEET | a group of fast booze boats, especially the contact boats that picked up liquor on Rum Row.

Appendix B
FLAPPER SLANG LANGUAGE

Flappers created their own slang language as a way to distinguish themselves from the previous "old-fashioned" generation. Here are some examples of flapper slang:

ALARM CLOCK (a.k.a. fire extinguisher) | a chaperone

ANCHOR | box of flowers

APPLE SAUCE | nonsense

BANK'S CLOSED | No kissing allowed

BEE'S KNEES (a.k.a. the BERRIES) | very nice, the best

BIG CHEESE | an important person (originated in this period)

BILLBOARD | flashy man or woman

BISCUIT | an impressionable flapper

BLOUSE | to go (i.e., "Let's blouse.")

BLOW | wild party

BLUSHING VIOLET | a publicity hound

BREEZER | a convertible car

BROOKSY | classy dresser

BUM'S RUSH | to be forced out of an establishment (originated in the early 1900s)

CAKE BASKET | a limousine

CARRY A TORCH | to have a crush on someone

CASH OR CHECK? | Do you want to kiss now or later?

CAT'S MEOW (a.k.a. CAT'S PAJAMAS) | the greatest, the best

CELLAR SMELLER | Prohibition enforcement officer

CLAM (aka CABBAGE) | a dollar

CLINGING VINES | women who cling to old-fashioned Victorian values

CLOTHESLINE | a flapper who can't keep a secret

COPACETIC | wonderful

CORN SHREDDER | a young man who dances on a girl's feet

DAPPER | a flapper's father

DARB | easy mark with a bankroll

DEAD SOLDIER | empty beer bottle

DIMBOX | a taxicab

DI MI | Goodness!

DINGLE DANGLER | One who insists on telephoning.

DOG KENNELS (a.k.a. ground grippers) | shoes

DON'T TAKE ANY WOODEN NICKELS | Don't do anything dumb.

DROPPING THE PILOT | getting a divorce

DUCKY | satisfactory, fine

DUDDING UP | dressing up

DUMB DORA | stupid girl

EDISONED | being asked a lot of questions.

EGG | a person who leads a wealthy, extravagant lifestyle (e.g., Jay Gatsby)

EMBALMER | a bootlegger

EYE OPENER | a marriage

FACE STRETCHER | old maid who tries to look young

FATHER TIME | any man over thirty years of age

FEATHERS | light conversation

FIRE ALARM | divorced woman

FIRE BELL | married woman

FLAP | girl

FLOP | going to bed

FLOUR LOVER | girl who powders too freely

FORTY-NINER | man prospecting for a rich wife

GIGGLE WATER | liquor, alcoholic beverage

GIMLET | a chronic bore

GIVE YOUR KNEE | cheek-to-cheek dancing

GO CHASE YOURSELF! | Get out of here!

GOLD-DIGGER | a female who engages in romantic relationships for money rather than love

GOOF | a flapper's steady

GOOFY | to be in love

GRUBBER | one who always borrows cigarettes

HALF-CUT | happily intoxicated

HANDCUFFS | engagement ring

HAYBURNER | a car with poor gas mileage, a gas guzzler

HEN COOP | a beauty parlor

HOOCH | liquor

HOTSEY TOTSEY | attractive

HOUDINI | to be on time for a date

HUSH MONEY | allowance from father

JAKE | OK, as in, "Everything is jake."

JOE | cup of coffee

JOHNNIE WALKER | guy who never hires a cab

JUICE JOINT | speakeasy

KNOW YOUR ONIONS | to know what's up or what's going on

LALAPAZAZER | a good sport

LAP | drink

LEMON SQUEEZER | an elevator or a subway car

LENS LOUISE | someone who monopolizes a conversation

MAD MONEY | carfare home if she has a fight with her escort

MANACLE | wedding ring

MEAT-BALL | dumb but happy

MRS. GRUNDY | an uptight or very strait-laced individual

MUNITIONS | face powder and rouge

NICE GIRL | one who takes a fellow in and introduces him to the family

NON-SKID | a girl who can carry her liquor

NOODLE JUICE | tea

NOW YOU'RE ON THE TROLLEY! | Now you've gotten it right!

OIL CAN | an unsophisticated person

OLIVER TWIST | an extremely good dancer

ORCHID | anything that is expensive

OSTRICH | anyone who thinks he knows it all

OUT ON PAROLE | a person who has been divorced

PILL | professor

POCKET TWISTER | girl who eats, dances and drinks up all of a man's spare change

POLICE DOG | young man to whom a flapper is engaged

REAL McCOY | the genuine article

ROCK OF AGES | any woman over thirty years of age

SHARPSHOOTER | one who spends well and dances freely

SHOW CASE | rich man's wife with her jewels

SLIMP | cheapskate

SMITH BROTHERS | guys who never cough up money

SMOKE EATER | a girl cigarette user

SNAKE CHARMER | female bootlegger

SOD BUSTER | an undertaker

SPIFFLICATED | inebriated

STATIC | conversation that means nothing

STEPPING OUT | reaching the flapper class

STILTS | legs

SWEETIE | anybody a flapper hates

TELL IT TO SWEENEY. | Tell it to someone who will believe your nonsense.

THEY | her parents

TOMATO | a young woman shy of brains (male version, POTATO)

UMBRELLA | young man any girl can borrow for the evening

WEASEL | girl stealer

WEEPING WILLOW | perpetual crier

WHANGDOODLE | jazz music, jazz band

WHISK BROOM | man with whiskers

WIND SUCKER | any person given to boasting

WURP | a person who is a buzzkill or wet blanket

ZOOZER | flapper who never spends a nickel

ZOZZLED | drunk

BIBLIOGRAPHY

Books

Canney, Donald L. *Rum War: The U.S. Coast Guard and Prohibition*. Washington, D.C.: U.S. Coast Guard, 1989.

Nellie Green's unfinished, unpublished manuscript (with Peter Cameron) 238 pages. Used with permission from the Green-Talmadge family.

Libraries and Archives

Blackstone Library (Branford, Connecticut). www.blackstonelibrary.org.

Boston Public Library, Leslie Jones Collection. www.bpl.org.

Branford Historical Society. www.branfordhistoricalsociety.org.

Bridgeport, TX Historical Society. www.bridgeporttxhistorical.org.

Bureau of Alcohol, Tobacco, Firearms and Explosives, Washington, D.C. www.atf.gov.

East Haven Historical Society. www.easthavenhistorical.webs.com/museum.

Fairfield Museum & History Center. www.fairfieldhistory.org.

J. Paul Getty Museum. https://www.getty.edu/museum.

Library of Congress. www.loc.gov.

Mariners' Museum and Park (Norfolk, Virginia). https://marinersmuseum.org.

National Archives. www.archives.gov.

Special Collections & University Archives, Pittsburg State University. https://axe.pittstate.edu/special-collections/index.html.

U.S. Coast Guard Academy Library. https://libguides.uscga.edu/home.

U.S. Coast Guard, New London, Connecticut. www.uscg.mil.

Walter P. Reuther Library, Archives of Labor and Urban Affairs, Wayne State University. www.reuther.wayne.edu.

Westport Historical Society. www.westporthistory.org.

Wisconsin Historical Society. www.wisconsinhistory.org.

Websites

Barnum Museum. www.barnum-museum.org.

Griswold Inn. www.griswoldinn.com.

Internet Movie Database. www.imdb.com.

Smugglers, Bootleggers and Scofflaws. "Raw Data on 250 Liquor Ships Seized during Prohibition near NYC." www.smugglersbootleggersandscofflaws.com/z-raw-data-rum-smugglers-nyc-1920-33.

State of Connecticut Public Document No. 26. www.portal.ct.gov/-/media/sots/ElectionServices/StatementOfVote_PDFs/1932SOVpdf.pdf?la=en.

Various newspapers. www.newspapers.com.

INDEX

ABOUT THE AUTHOR

Tony Renzoni is the author of the well-received books *Connecticut Rock 'n' Roll: A History* and *Connecticut Softball Legend Joan Joyce*, both published by The History Press.

Tony had a thirty-eight-year career with the federal government. As district manager in Connecticut's Fairfield County, he oversaw the operations of four field offices, serving over 100,000 beneficiaries. Tony wrote over one thousand weekly columns that were published in the *Connecticut Post* newspaper and on the paper's website. Tony was a recipient of more than forty awards, including his agency's highest honor award.

A lifelong resident of Connecticut, Tony lives on the Connecticut shoreline with his wife, Colleen. Tony Renzoni is a graduate of Waterbury's Sacred Heart High School and Sacred Heart University in Fairfield, Connecticut.

Visit us at
www.historypress.com
....